Dedicated to
MONSIGNOR JOHN J. EGAN,
priest and prophet

Liturgy and Social Justice

Edited by
Mark Searle

THE LITURGICAL PRESS, Collegeville, Minnesota

Nihil obstat: Joseph C. Kremer, S.T.L., *Censor deputatus.*
Imprimatur: ✝George H. Speltz, D.D., Bishop of St. Cloud. October 11, 1980.

Library of Congress Cataloging in Publication Data

Main entry under title:

Liturgy and social justice.

1. Liturgics — Catholic Church — Addresses, essays, lectures. 2. Social justice — Addresses, essays, lectures. 3. Catholic Church — Addresses, essays, lectures. I. Searle, Mark, 1941–
BX1970.L499   264'.02   80-27011
ISBN 0-8146-1209-1 (pbk.)

Contents

Abbreviations

AAS   *Acta Apostolicae Sedis.* Rome, 1909–.

GS   *Gaudium et spes,* Pastoral Constitution on the Church in the Modern World. Vatican II, December 7, 1965.

LG   *Lumen gentium,* Dogmatic Constitution on the Church. Vatican II, November 21, 1964.

Mansi   J. D. Mansi, ed., *Sacrorum Conciliorum nova et amplissima collectio.* 31 vols. Florence-Venice 1757–98.

MD   *Mediator Dei.* Pius XII, November 20, 1947.

PL   *Patrologia Latina,* ed. J. P. Migne. Paris 1844–64.

TDNT   *Theological Dictionary of the New Testament,* ed. G. Kittel, trans. G. W. Bromiley. Grand Rapids, Mich. 1964–74.

Foreword

Some books fill a precise need; this is one of them. Both the history of social ministry in the Church and its theology since Vatican II point to the need for a systematic address to the relationship of social ministry and worship.

The historical relationship of the liturgical movement and social ministry in the United States during the first half of this century illustrates the potential of one dimension of the Church's life to enrich the other. One of my first approaches to the systematic study of Catholic social teaching came through reading the *Proceedings* of the Liturgical Conference. In those volumes the names of Godfrey Diekmann, O.S.B., Reynold Hillenbrand, Shawn Sheehan, H. A. Reinhold and Bill Leonard, S.J., complemented those of John A. Ryan, Bishop Haas, George Higgins and Jack Egan. The theme of the Church as the Body of Christ was elaborated in terms of the Church at worship and the Church in witness. The resources were solid in quality but sparse in quantity. The key texts were *Mystici Corporis, Mediator Dei,* and the social teaching of Leo XIII, Pius XI, and Pius XII. From these texts was fashioned a theological basis for a style of worship with a strong social consciousness and a style of social ministry rooted in the sacraments. Not least of the achievements of this theology was a growing affirmation of the yet unacknowledged but essential role of the laity in worship and witness.

The work of the 1940s and 1950s, here and elsewhere in the Church, bore fruit in the conciliar years of the 1960s. What had been called "movements" (i.e., on the margin of the Church's life) became the central resources of the conciliar agenda. The

9

theological development manifested in the conciliar documents was impressive: from *Mystici Corporis* to *The Constitution on the Church;* from *Mediator Dei* to *The Constitution on the Sacred Liturgy;* and from a disparate, developing literature on social ministry to the rich "surprise document" of the Council, *The Pastoral Constitution on the Church in the Modern World.* The Council provided the framework for the diverse movements of the 1940s and 50s to become central strands in the fabric of Catholic faith at the level of theological reflection and Christian life.

Fifteen years after the Council this potential remains largely unfulfilled in the Church in the United States. This is not a statement about what has happened in each area of Church life. There has been substantial change and development in liturgy, ecclesiology, and social ministry. What has yet to be achieved is what John Courtney Murray once called the work of systematization required by the Council. Systematization at the theological level means integration at the level of lived experience in the Church. The dialogue of different dimensions of the Church's life that characterized the preconciliar pages of the Liturgical Conference's *Proceedings* has not been well cultivated in the post-conciliar period. It was perhaps inevitable that the resources of the Council in each distinct area had to be worked out for a while. But now integration is the demand of the moment, intellectually and experientially. For if, as Pope John Paul II stated at Puebla, the Church's "evangelizing mission has as an essential part action for justice," then such action surely must be rooted in the liturgy that Vatican II called the summit and source of Christian life.

The task of systematization and integration is multidimensional. It is a work of intellectual acumen and organizational skill. These chapters address the theological linkage between social ministry and liturgical life. The authors bring meticulous scholarship and pastoral sensitivity to a task requiring both. The need for this book is evident to anyone interested in liturgy that nourishes life. It is equally evident to those who see justice and peace as both human tasks and, at the same time, signs of the Kingdom among us. This book meets a need that many see and feel today. It is fitting that The Liturgical Press, so long a source of both social justice and liturgical themes, should be the publisher, and Notre Dame University, a center of social and liturgical ministry today, should be the source of the book.

J. Bryan Hehir
United States Catholic Conference

Serving the Lord with Justice

MARK SEARLE

In a thirteenth-century version of the legend of the Holy Grail, the story is told of how the poor knight Parsifal stumbles upon the castle where the Grail is kept. For miles around, the land lies desolate. Within the castle Parsifal finds a company burdened with sadness, surrounding a king suffering from a mysterious wound. Parsifal watches in amazement as first the bloody Lance and then the life-giving Grail are carried before him. He is disturbed by the strange suffering of the people, but he asks no questions. The next morning he awakes to find the castle deserted; the wounded king and all his sorrowful court have disappeared, and with them the Holy Grail.

A long time later, after years of fruitless adventuring and after forty days of penance, Parsifal is given a second chance. He returns to the castle a changed and chastened man. Now, humbly, he is moved to ask two questions: "What is your sorrow?" and "Whom does one serve in serving the Grail?" He is given no answer to his questions — it is enough that he asks them. The afflicted king is immediately healed, the people sense the lifting of a great burden of misery, and the land itself bursts into life.

MARK SEARLE is associate director of the Notre Dame Center for Pastoral Liturgy and assistant professor of liturgical studies at the University of Notre Dame. This paper was the major address at the eighth annual Notre Dame Conference on Pastoral Liturgy, June 1979.

The quest for the Grail is a famous and powerful symbol of the quest for the source of life itself, of the search for wholeness and healing, of the quest for God. The release of its power affects not simply the wounds of the stricken king but the vitality of the land and the well-being of the people as a whole.

There has always been a certain tension between the inner life and social reform. On occasion the dichotomy has been transcended by mystics who were also social reformers, but the history of Christianity is for the most part a history of vacillation between contemplation and action, as first one and then the other has enjoyed higher esteem. At times, matters of charity and social justice have appeared to be at best appendages to the really important business of saving one's soul or even as means to that higher end. At other times, including perhaps our own, recognition of the practical and social implications of Christian commitment have rendered the cultivation of the spiritual life suspect as a kind of self-indulgent luxury.

The story of Parsifal offers us a symbolic image in which pursuit of the Grail and concern for the suffering neighbor are intrinsically and inseparably connected, without either being reduced to the other. We have to ask of the needy, "What is your sorrow?" Yet, at the same time we must also raise the question, "Whom does one serve in serving the Grail?"[1] It is not so much a matter of the first question relating to the active dimension of Christian life and the second to its contemplative dimension, for the Grail is a symbol of total healing — personal, social, spiritual, and communal. Somehow the questions are more closely linked than that. Each is a dimension of the other, and we want to explore how that might be the case, and particularly why the liturgy is important for Christians committed to social justice.

I. Justice in Liturgy and in Christian Life

Let us begin with a clarification of terms. In the first place, "liturgy" means much more than texts or rubrics; it comprises the whole event of a Christian community gathering to celebrate the rituals of the Church. The term is used here as referring to the actions of a gathered community in hearing the Word of God, breaking bread, initiating new members, anointing the sick, celebrating conversion and renewal, marrying and giving in marriage, ordaining its leaders, or joining together in the praise and acknowledgment of God.

The question we want to ask is this: What has all this liturgical activity to do with the cause of justice? For some people, the answer would be "Nothing." Others would see an indirect link insofar as they believe that churchgoing is a stabilizing influence in society and that religion helps people to keep the law and to live as conscientious citizens. Others again would like to see religion more explicitly endorse specific political options, and the ritual of the Church take on the role of deliberate social consciousness-raising.

Part of what is at stake here, of course, is the question of the larger relationship between personal beliefs and social engagement, but there are also different concepts of justice involved. Whatever people's social philosophy might be, justice very often comes down to what the law defines as just or unjust; or, where the law itself is deemed inadequate or unjust, it comes down to what the Constitution can be argued to provide. In short, in a pluralistic society such as ours, where agreement upon any kind of absolute principles is virtually impossible to achieve, justice in fact means legal justice, and the struggle for justice means seeking legal redress or Constitutional amendment for situations felt to be unjust.[2] Even basic human rights have to be argued as a matter of positive law when arguments over them take the form of an appeal to the law or to the Constitution or to international agreements.

But it would be confusing to look to the liturgy for support or insight in the pursuit of legal arguments, for the justice that it celebrates, while not unrelated, is fundamentally of a very different kind. The liturgy celebrates the justice of God himself, as revealed by him in history, recorded in the Scriptures, and proclaimed in the assembly of the faithful. This is not the kind of justice that consists in arbitrating between conflicting claims or enforcing observance of legal codes. Not that such things are any the less important for that, for, as Robert Bolt's Thomas More knew full well, we must often seek refuge from tyranny in the thickets of the law.[3] What this does suggest, however, is that the justice of the law or of the Constitution or of the Geneva Convention cannot simply be identified with the justice of God; and it is with his justice that the liturgy is concerned.

For its own part, the justice of God is not to be understood, as it often is in the popular imagination at least, as a matter of legal enactment or as the expression of a certain divine wisdom in tailoring exquisitely fitting punishment to the crimes of the inescapably guilty. The justice of God is ultimately God himself, just as he is. It is a justice that is revealed in all that God does to reveal himself. In creation it is revealed by things being the way he made them and serving the purpose for which they were made. In history God's justice is manifest in the people and events that embody and fulfill his will. In short, the justice of God is satisfied when things conform to the purpose for which he made them. (And this would suggest, incidentally, that questions of beauty and authenticity are, for the Judeo-Christian tradition, not simply matters of personal taste but of God's justice.)

Human justice, it might be said, is at best a bridle on evil; God's justice is the flowering of the good. That is why God's justice must transcend legal justice: "I tell you, if your justice goes no deeper than that of the scribes and the Pharisees, you will never get into the kingdom of heaven" (Matt 5:20). God's justice is done when arbitration is transformed by reconciliation; when people become more than objects of desire, manipulation, and profit; when poverty is confronted by asking, not how much the poor require, but how much the rich need; when the goods of the earth are looked upon, not as sources of private profit, but as sacraments of divine and human intercommunication. As and when such things occur, however rarely or fleetingly, then God's justice is done, and there the rule or Kingdom of God becomes manifest. For the justice of God that the liturgy proclaims *is* the Kingdom of God.

It is true that the reign of justice in this sense is at best intermittently realized in human history and that its full and definitive realization awaits the parousia, but it is a matter of hope, not just of vague optimism. It is a matter of hope because it has already happened. The justice of God has been revealed among us in many and various ways throughout the course of human history, but above all it has been seen in all its dimensions in the person of Jesus. He was the Just One. He not only spoke about the coming Kingdom, speculatively as it were, but he embodied it in his own person. In his life and activity he modeled the radically different justice which is that of the Kingdom of God. By living and dying in total accord with his Father's will and by doing all he did in fulfillment of the Father's intentions for the world, Jesus lived the justice of God. He was a just man, not because he kept the law, but because he lived according to the order and vocation of the One who predetermines all things. Not surprisingly, this brought him into conflict with contemporary systems of justice in his own society. But the fact that such divine justice has been realized in human form upon this earth means that it is no escapist utopia but a real possibility and the object of a well-founded hope. And the fact that the same Spirit that animated him has been poured out upon the rest of humanity means that the realization of such justice may henceforth always be looked for and worked for.

In every generation some people are called by name consciously to serve this Kingdom and its justice as revealed in Jesus. They are called Christians, and together, as a new humanity, they have the unenviable responsibility of representing the hope of a higher justice and working for its realization. It is not that the Kingdom and justice of God are to be found only

among them, but they are called and commissioned in its service. The form in which they receive that commission is the ritual
known as baptism, in which they are called to surrender themselves to the God who revealed himself in Jesus and whom they
acknowledge as the Creator of the world and the Lord of
history. These disciples of Jesus, who die to the man-made and
demonically disjointed world of their times, begin to live according to a new order and according to a new principle: the Spirit of
God who enables them to do the works of God.

The position of these disciples is well summarized in the words
of an anonymous early apologist:

> Christians are not distinguished from the rest of mankind by
> either country, speech, or customs; the fact is, they nowhere set-
> tle in cities of their own; they use no peculiar language; they
> cultivate no eccentric mode of life. . . . Yet, while they settle in
> both Greek and non-Greek cities, as each one's lot is cast, and
> conform to the customs of the country in dress, diet, and mode of
> life in general, the whole tenor of their way of living stamps it as
> worthy of admiration and contrary to expectation. . . . They
> spend their days on earth, but hold citizenship in heaven. They
> obey the established laws, but in their private lives go beyond the
> law. They love all and are persecuted by all. . . . They are poor
> and enrich many. . . .

This same writer goes on to summarize the position of the Christians by saying:

> . . . what the soul is in the body, that the Christians are in the
> world. . . . Such is the important post to which God has as-
> signed them, and it is not lawful for them to desert it.[4]

Politics has been defined as the art of the possible, but the post
to which God has assigned Christians goes far beyond this.
What is possible or realistic or prudent for the unconverted is, as
we are too well aware, not very much. In this new order,
however, we are called to live beyond our own very real limita-
tions. By virtue of the Spirit of God, it is possible to offer
hospitality to strangers, to do good without charge, to share

one's bread, to care for the afflicted without seeking to profit from another's misfortune, to exercise authority in a way that invites free assent instead of compelling grudging conformity. These may not appear to be great matters, but they illustrate in a simple and traditional way the sort of thing that the justice of the world cannot demand but the justice of God requires.

Perhaps this was why, in the third century,[5] the criteria for deciding whether apparent converts were really being called by God to this community of witness were simply: Have they, after being in contact with the Church, learned to live an honest life? Have they honored the widows? Have they cared for the sick? Have they shown themselves assiduous in doing good? In translation that might read: Have they come to appreciate the new justice? Have they learned to share their surplus? Have they had their eyes opened to the egotism of a consumer society? Have they learned to overcome the cannibalistic individualism of the age and put themselves at the service of the needy and oppressed?

Yet it is important to understand the motivation of this new order. These were not "do-gooders," working out their own problems under the guise of helping others. They were more like reformed alcoholics: people whose conversion to justice had inevitably confronted them with their own injustice and poverty. Once they had been caught up, as victims and perpetrators, in the injustice of the world, but then they had experienced the liberating power of God's justice. That liberating justice of God continued to operate in history in the daily life and work of Christian people. The power of God's justice, which lifts up the lowly and undermines the pretensions of the powerful, was recognized both in the shape of the community's worship and in the shape of its common life. The two were not separable: both liturgy and the events of daily life were equally occasions for bearing generous and faithful testimony to the fact that God's merciful justice finds its scope in human history.

The close continuity between liturgical celebration and social

action is evident in the early history of the liturgy. It was the role
of the bishop not only to preside at the liturgy and to preach but
also to oversee the general welfare of his people and to involve
himself directly in settling disputes, feeding the poor, caring for
the sick, providing for orphans and widows. In this he was
helped by deacons and deaconesses, whose social role was likewise carried over into the community celebration. One might
also mention the merging of liturgy and life in such matters as
the holding of agapes, the importance attached to the collection,
the care and anointing of the sick, the formation of cate-
chumens, and the institution of public penance and public reconciliation for grave sins.

Moreover, given that the concept of *anamnesis* meant more
than simply remembering the past and implied a real participation in the events remembered, the Eucharistic prayers, too, may
be read as testimony to the continuing experience of God's saving justice. A common appellation of God in the Eucharistic
prayers of the East is "lover of the human race." Thus the account of the *mirabilia Dei*, especially as it focuses on the life of
Christ, constitutes not only an account of the past works of
God's justice but an implicit program for the ongoing life of the
Christian community.

One Egyptian anaphora, the Alexandrian anaphora of
Gregory Nazianzen,[6] speaks of the *mirabilia Dei* as having been
wrought among, and on behalf of, the worshiping community;
this sense of intimacy and immediacy is emphasized by the
prayer being offered largely in the first person singular and
punctuated throughout by the congregation's cries of *Kyrie
eleison*. The proclamation of God's mighty works is brought to a
conclusion and tied into the institution narrative with the words,
"I offer you the symbols of this my liberty . . . ." This liberation, which is the freedom enjoyed by the praying community, is
attributed to him who has been acclaimed as the "lover of the
human race." It is a liberty wrought both in the saving acts of
God in the past and realized in the ongoing life of Christian peo-

ple, for the justice of God continues to bless and redeem the earth through the lives of those who love him and acknowledge him.

II. Justice as Revealed in the Liturgy

We have seen that the liturgy celebrates the justice of God as revealed above all in Jesus, and we have further suggested that such justice prevails when the will of God is done: when the relationships that God intends to exist within his creation, and between his creation and himself, do in fact exist. This is not a justice, then, that begins with human rights abstractly conceived, but with a divine economy in process of realization. It starts with a God-given order in which everything is assigned its rightful place or, better, with a divine teleology in which all created things are called to fulfill their rightful purpose and destiny under God.

It is probably true to say that, given the unfolding and always incomplete understanding of our purpose and destiny, it is easier to recognize injustice than it is to say precisely and specifically what the Kingdom of God demands under all circumstances. Nevertheless, the liturgy does reveal, at least in outline, the positive dimensions of the Kingdom and indicates the kind of God-given relationships that constitute the justice of the Kingdom. These relationships are of three kinds: our relationship with God, our relationship with one another, and our relationship with material creation.

1. Our Relationship with God

Every Eucharistic liturgy contains at least one clear and apodictic statement about justice; it occurs at the beginning of the Eucharistic prayer:

> Let us give thanks to the Lord our God.
> It is right to give him thanks and praise.

Vere dignum et iustum est . . . tibi gratias agere: it really is

right, it is a matter of justice, that we should always and everywhere give you thanks. In view of this sentiment, which belongs
to the original and indispensable core of the Eucharistic liturgy,
it is hardly surprising that St. Thomas Aquinas should have seen
the virtue of religion as a part of the moral virtue of justice. "He
is our unfailing source and to him more than to any other we
must be bound; he is our last end and to him our choice must be
constantly directed; it is God whom we spurn and lose when we
sin; it is God whom we must regain once more by believing in
him and pledging our loyalty to him."[7] Significantly enough,
Pius XII took this quotation from St. Thomas as the starting
point for his encyclical on the liturgy, *Mediator Dei* (1947).

The Christian liturgy, true to its ancestry in the Jewish
berakoth, acknowledges the God who created and sustains the
universe and who has intervened as Savior in the course of
human history to shape it to its proper end. Thus the liturgy proclaims God as the source of all justice in his own being, a justice
that has been revealed both in creation and in history and that
has gained for him the accolade "lover of the human race." So it
is that the official prayer of the Christian community begins
each new day with the invitation:

> Come, then, let us bow down and worship,
>   bending the knee before the Lord, our maker,
> For he is our God and we are his people,
>   the flock he shepherds.[8]

Such acknowledgment of God is basic to the Judeo-Christian
prayer tradition, finding expression in the Jewish *berakoth*, or
blessings, and in the major prayers of all the Christian sacraments. But it is also essential to the cause of justice, and this for
two reasons.

First, the acknowledgment of the absolute claim of God and of
his justice as something that transcends any historical attempt to
be faithful to such a claim relativizes all social programs, all
political systems, and all just causes. The Kingdom of God is

certainly present among us, but it is not to be identified with any particular form of the social order or with any given political system. For this reason no form of government, no program of reform, can ever claim absolute rights over individuals or communities, no matter how good and beneficial it might appear to be; and no institution or cause can claim the total and unquestioning loyalty of any person. When they do make such claims, they become demonic, arrogating to themselves what belongs properly to God alone. We must join institutions and movements, but we may not sell out to them. Thus, acknowledgment of the absolute claim of God's justice becomes a source of critical consciousness vis-à-vis all political and social programs.

Second, the acknowledgment that the work of justice — the work of liberation, development, and reconciliation — is the work of God must save us from any messiah complex. The Christian must necessarily engage in such work, but the cause is God's, as are the power and the glory. Without this sort of conscious awareness and the humility it entails, there is always the grave danger of people imposing their own ideas and ambitions upon the less fortunate, further compromising their freedom and condemning both the would-be helper and the client to eventual disillusionment and perhaps despair. Thus, acknowledgment of the transcendent source and goal of all justice becomes a source of critical self-awareness for all who would commit themselves to the service of others.[9]

2. Relationships in the Human Community

We have seen that relationships within the human community are themselves affected by the existential awareness (or lack of awareness) of who it is we serve. For the Christian — so the prayer of the liturgy would suggest — the motivation for philanthropic work is one's own profound awareness of the divine philanthropy. We stand to one another not as the rich to the poor, the wise to the ignorant, the strong to the needy, the clever to the simple; we stand rather as the poor to the poor, the weak to the weak, the loved to the loved. The history of charitable, political, and social enterprises is full of instances of paternalism, manipulation, and exploitation inflicted upon the unfortunate in the name of good. Power corrupts and knowledge inflates, unless the power and the knowledge are recognized as gifts over which we have only stewardship, not ownership. We are not the leaders; we all belong to the flock that is led by God's hand.

Moreover, for the members of the worshiping community, relationships with one's fellow human beings are based not simply upon their common humanity but upon their common humanity as assumed and redeemed by the love and obedience of Jesus, and raised to a new level by the Spirit of Jesus at work in the world. This realization makes the believers' love for one another not just a vague ethical imperative, but an expression of the new life to which they have, by no merits of their own, been reborn and which is essentially communal. It is in the actual historical community into which they have been incorporated by baptism that the new life is to be worked out and brought to full realization in the perfected personhood of each of the children of God. This happens, as does all personal development, through interaction in which each person's unique combination of gifts is called forth in response to others. The liturgical assembly, at least in its ideal form, offers a model of such interaction. It is not a community of equals but a community of God-given and complementary charisms, gifts that cannot be identified *a priori* by the categories of the secular community—age, sex, race—but are distributed by God indiscriminately among all for the sole purpose of building up the community in perfect justice.

Furthermore, the work of the Spirit to renew the face of the earth is different from his creation of the material world in that it calls for the free response of every person, inviting each to surrender to the liberating will of God in the community of the human family. The work of the Spirit is intensely personal and thoroughly liberating. As such, it saves us from the chilling anonymity of clienthood and the faceless inhumanity of being reduced to a statistic—people are not just cases to be counted, documented, and processed. The experience of God's justice as grace and gift might also save us from compelling people to accept help they do not want, or to submit to programs designed without their consultation, or to accept new forms of dependency upon those who claim to be liberating them. (It is perhaps because the Church has not always recognized the existential freedom which grace brings that she has submitted people to moral, economic, and even physical compulsion in the name of the gospel, while theologians sipped tea and debated the niceties of prevenient grace and free will.)

To put the matter more positively, the liturgy presupposes a group of people who can reach across the social, political, and economic barriers that structure our world to say "Our Father" and to speak of themselves as "we." Such a community, even in its liturgical manifestations, is unable to realize perfectly all the demands of justice. For that to happen, it would have to be truly universal and truly particular, intimate enough for all to know one another and to accept one another profoundly, and at the same time open to all and sundry without exception. In fact, as we know only too well, the liturgical assembly reflects, not the justice of the Kingdom, but the divisions of social groupings. That is the torment and the tension of being confronted with the Kingdom in the assembly of the faithful, but the tension has to be retained. Justice is properly a mark of the Church, like her being one, holy, catholic, and apostolic. Like these other qualities, it constitutes a tension rather than an achievement; something given, yet always to be realized. If that tension is relaxed, however, the Christian community falls from the justice of God and relapses into the thoughtless acceptance of an unjust world, taking as normal and unexceptionable the ambitions of power, the maldistribution of wealth, and the social and racial divisions that characterize our world.

3. Relationship to Material Creation

The justice of God, as it finds expression in the quality of human relationships, has everything to do with his justice as it affects the goods of the earth. Material goods are not just neutral objects, but, as our economic system makes us aware, they are the mediators of human relationships. As valuables, items of necessity, usefulness, or luxury; as fruits of labor, marketable commodities, cherished possessions, or desirable acquisitions, they represent not themselves alone, but the values and aspirations and experiences of the human community of users. It was as such that they were intended from the beginning. The goods of the earth were set at our disposal to be transformed, through manufacture and use, into vehicles of human communication and carriers of human meaning. Perhaps we see this most clearly with gifts. A gift is not just an object, a thing; it bespeaks the giver and conveys to the recipient, not just the transfer of ownership and use, but the bond of a relationship.

When God, according to Genesis, created the world, saw that it was good, and then entrusted it to the human race, it was to serve the ongoing development of that race into a community of mutual exchange and growing complicity. Yet all material goods put into human hands immediately acquire a certain ambivalence. They can be used to build up relationships as God intended, or they can be turned into instruments of division and violence. Everything, from a piece of rock to nuclear energy, has the capacity to be used constructively or destructively. Unless material creation is recognized as belonging to its Creator, with a meaning and destiny that derive from the place assigned to it in his historical economy, it becomes the mute victim of our lust for possession and of our egotistical will to power. What was meant to speak to us of God and to further our ties with one another now becomes a matter of personal possession, arbitrary exploitation, and alienated self-sufficiency.

But when Jesus took bread and wine or a few fish and blessed God for them and shared them with his disciples, creation found its purpose once again.[10] When the wood of the Cross, itself the innocent victim and unchoosing collaborator in man's inhumanity to man, became the means of expressing a hitherto undreamed of relationship between God and his people, the wood itself was redeemed. In each instance the true order of things was restored and justice reigned insofar as created things could now once again speak of God, the "lover of the human race." At the same time, and inseparably, they spoke of the right relationship that should exist between human beings. When Jesus took the bread, said the blessing, broke the bread and shared it, he demonstrated, unforgettably, the proper use of all material things. The early Christians realized this: they "eucharistized" their lives by blessing God in all things and by making their possessions available to one another. And when Jesus took the cup and gave thanks to God and passed it among his disciples, he rediscovered for the human race the joy of not claiming anything for one's own — not even life itself.

It used to be thought that the "matter" of the sacraments was bread, wine, oil, water, and so forth. More recently there has been a healthy tendency to suggest that it is not bread that constitutes the sacramental sign of the Eucharist, nor oil that is the sacramental sign of confirmation or anointing of the sick, but bread that is broken and shared, the cup of wine passed around for all to drink, the oil applied by one person to another. The sacraments are actions of the body, through which we become present to one another and touch one another's lives. Thus, created realities, including in the first place the human body, find their fulfillment in being used to build up the human community in accordance with the designs of God.

Creation, groaning to be redeemed from the homicidal perversions to which our sinful use has subjected it, finds its liberation when it is used as it is used in the liturgy: to acknowledge and express the justice of God in the midst of his people, who are being bonded into a community by their common and respectful use of material things. Over against that stand all forms of selfish appropriation and misuse of created realities, an appropriation and abuse that seem inseparable from unjust relationships between people. It is a long way from Cain's murder of Abel to the stockpiling of nuclear armaments or the mutual exploitation of Western capitalism, but the simplest celebration of the Eucharist, the breaking of bread, cries out against the normalization and rationalization of injustice in the use of material goods, and against the way we turn the creation committed to our care into weapons of power and destruction.

III. Liturgy as Social Criticism

It has been argued here that the justice proclaimed in the liturgy is the justice of God and of his Kingdom. Further, such justice involves right relationships between human beings and God, between human beings themselves as individuals and as communities, and between human beings and material creation. Such relationships are right insofar as they allow each party to be what it is: allowing God to be God, human beings to be human, and creation, whether animate or inanimate, to be treated gratefully and respectfully. Moreover, the justice of God and the integrity of the human person are such that failure in one set of relationships constitutes a failure in all—justice is indivisible.

All this may sound idealistic and remote, indeed so remote as to be useless as a guide to action. On the other hand, the justice of God presented in the liturgy is anything but an abstraction, for the liturgy of the Church sacramentalizes the presence of Christ, the Just One. For that reason, and for that reason alone, we can say that the liturgy not only proclaims the justice of the Kingdom of God as something to be done but actually renders it present, not as an achievement of ours but as a gift of God. In its presence we are confronted with that which we are called to be, with that which God would make us be, if we permit it. Thus the liturgy not only provides us with a moral ideal but confronts us with an ontological reality in the light of which the ambivalence of our own lives is revealed for what it is.

Like the Word of God in history, the liturgy is the revelation of God's justice in both event and word, cutting into human life both as good news and as denunciation. It proclaims and realizes the saving presence of the Spirit in the world, brings the presence of the Kingdom, and enables us to realize where this is happening even outside the liturgy. Celebrating the liturgy should train us to recognize justice and injustice when we see it. It serves as a basis for social criticism by giving us a criterion by which to evaluate the events and structures of the world. But it is not just the world "out there" that stands under the judgment of God's justice, sacramentally realized in the liturgy. The first accused is the Church itself, which, to the degree that it fails to recognize what it is about, eats and drinks condemnation to itself (1 Cor 11:29).

In saying "Amen" to the justice of God proclaimed in the liturgy, we are implicitly saying "Anathema" to all that fails to measure up to that justice. Perhaps we need on occasion to make that explicit. Perhaps we need in the liturgy not only ways of saying "Amen — so be it; that is as it should be," but also ways of saying "This should not be, this must not be!" Maybe we need to borrow, as the old Book of Common Prayer did, the liturgical comminations or curses of Deuteronomy:

> A curse on him who treats his father or mother
> dishonorably. . . .
> A curse on him who displaces his neighbor's boundary
> mark. . . .
> A curse on him who leads a blind man astray on the road. . . .
> A curse on him who tampers with the rights of the stranger,
> the orphan and the widow. . . . (Deut 27:16-19).

But while the liturgy does provide us with a basis for social criticism, it neither dispenses with the need for policy planning and programs of social action nor provides us with any specific guidelines for setting about such undertakings. Consequently, Christians as such can claim no special gifts of practical wisdom or infused knowledge in the political arena. On the other hand, they are equipped by the gospel and the liturgy with a sense of the overall meaning and direction of the struggle for justice and with an ideal (the Kingdom) which, while its positive dimensions may be difficult to spell out in specific terms, at least enables us to evaluate critically the direction and value of our work and the attitudes out of which we operate. The liturgy provides a model or ideal in the light of which all human justice is judged and all mere lip service to God is itself denounced as injustice.

It would be misleading to look to the liturgy, as it would be to look to the Scriptures, for detailed prescriptions for dealing with contemporary problems.[11] On the other hand, while the liturgy does serve as a negative criterion for recognizing injustice in all its forms, it also has a more positive function. It functions, I would suggest, as an enacted parable.

The point about a parable is that when its character as parable is recognized, it is characteristically non-directive. Thus, the story that Jesus tells in response to a question or to a particular situation is one whose unexpected contrasts enable the listeners to come to an entirely different perspective concerning the matter at hand.[12] Having come to that new point of view, they are then left free to decide how to react. It is typical of Jesus — and therefore of God's justice — that he does not attempt to force people in a particular direction but invites them to discover the true dimensions of the Kingdom and to act accordingly. By opening up new horizons, Jesus allows his hearers to exercise their freedom in a more complete way. (One might add that the meals of Jesus recorded in the Scriptures have this same characteristic and may be understood as enacted parables of the Kingdom.) The liturgy, then, is intended, like the parables of Jesus, to generate insight and to offer a call rather than to impose moral imperatives; or rather, the moral imperative arises from within the person as a free and personal response to the insight that Jesus gives.

What is true of the parables and parabolic situations of Jesus in the Gospels is true for the liturgy also, though the liturgy has generally suffered the same fate as the parables in the hands of preachers and teachers, in being moralized and used to prove an ethical point. Yet the liturgy retains its parabolic potential to subvert all human perspectives and to offer us a way of seeing the world from the vantage point of God's justice revealed in word and sacrament. We are left to draw our own conclusions, or rather, we are left as a community to decide what appropriate forms of action might be called for in view of the newly recognized disparity between the order ordained by God and the order that actually prevails. The parable of the mustard seed, for example, retold in a large, anonymous congregation, might generate one set of insights; in a small, impoverished, and perhaps persecuted community it would generate others. The exercise of assembling for Eucharist, or the gesture of breaking the bread, will likewise generate insights of different kinds in different situations. The insight is generated by the contrast between what is and what might be, between the story of the participants and the story implied in the rite.

Another important parallel between the liturgy and the parables of Jesus is to be found in the fact that Jesus not only told parables but also engaged in parabolic actions, for example eating and drinking with sinners. This makes it easier to recognize the parabolic character of the liturgy, insofar as liturgy is not a text but an event; not an object but a participatory activity; not a story told but a drama enacted. Thus it shares the same function as the actions of Christ, namely, that of being not just a description of what the Kingdom of God is like, but the very presence of that Kingdom and its justice in the person and action of Christ, now present sacramentally in the assembly of the faithful. "Do this . . . . ," Jesus said, referring to the parable we call Eucharist. In doing it, justice is done and the Kingdom is present sacramentally, for all sacramental acts are the actions of Christ, the Just One. Their effectiveness depends upon the eruption into time of the eschatological reign of God's justice as a real and present gift; and it depends upon the community's appropriation of that gift, that is, making that justice its own.

The liturgical assembly, then, is the place where justice is proclaimed, but it is neither a classroom nor a political rally nor a hearing. It is more like a rehearsal room where actions must be repeated over and over until they are thoroughly assimilated and perfected—until, that is, the actors have totally identified with the part assigned to them. The liturgical action is a rehearsal of the utopian Kingdom first enacted upon the human stage in the meals that Jesus shared with outcasts and sinners. In it we learn to understand the drama of God's justice as it unfolds in our world and to identify with the role assigned to us so that we may play it effectively in our lives and eventually before the throne of God for all eternity, when his justice will be established beyond all compromise.

This, of course, is not to say that every liturgical celebration is a triumph of divine justice—we are obviously far from it. But the nature of the sacraments is such that, where the Church celebrates them as Christ intends, the justice of the Kingdom is more or less apparent for those who have eyes to see and ears to hear and allow themselves to be drawn into it. On the other hand, when the community fails to practice justice, it fails to celebrate as Christ intended. Then we have the laconic and chilling verdict of Paul: "It is not the Lord's Supper that you are eating" (1 Cor 11:20).

Conclusion: The Exaltation of Justice

At the beginning of this essay, the question was posed as to why the liturgy might be important to Christians committed to social justice. Perhaps the foregoing reflections can offer some hints as to an answer. It should be clear, however, that while not every Christian is necessarily called to become a social activist in the usual sense of that term, no one can safely celebrate the liturgy who is indifferent to the claims of God's justice upon the world or who is not willing, in Paul's terms, to offer his or her living body as a sacrifice by breaking with the injustice of the world (Rom 12:1ff.). For it is in the nature of the liturgy that it presents us with the Kingdom of God and draws us into its justice.

In other words, liturgy and justice go together because they are both going in the same direction: Godward. The Christian vision does not allow for pulling in two directions, one vertical and the other horizontal. In Christ these opposites are reconciled. Henceforth there is movement only in one direction: toward God our future. The word of justice has issued from his mouth and is now returning to him enfleshed in humanity. For this reason we can agree with Alexander Schmemann when he writes:

> Christianity falls down as soon as the idea of our going up in Christ's ascension – the movement of sacrifice – begins to be replaced with his going down. And that is exactly where we are today: it is always a bringing him down into ordinary life, and this we say will solve our social problems. The Church must go down to the ghetto, into the world in all its reality. But to save the world from social injustices, the need first of all is not to go down to its miseries, as to have a few witnesses in this world to its possible ascension.[13]

The Christian attitude toward the world, then, is not one of condescension, but one of witnessing to the hope of exaltation. This hope is realistic only insofar as it is experienced, but it is experienced only by those who have learned to recognize the disparity between the values of the Kingdom and the values by which our world is organized, and who have learned to surrender to the former and break with the latter.

Dostoyevsky expressed a similar point of view in his novel *The Brothers Karamazov*.[14] Satan admits to Ivan Karamazov that if he, Satan, had only been able to bring himself to shout "Hosanna!" when the Son of Man was ascending into heaven, history would have come to an end. What did Dostoyevsky mean by this? Presumably that if injustice, which he personifies in the best liturgical tradition as Satan, had acknowledged the sovereignty of God, the Kingdom would no longer have been contested, opposition to it would have ceased, and the world as we know it would have passed. It is an idea not far removed from the belief that if every Jew observed the Torah for one day, the Messiah would come; for if every Jew submitted to the justice of God, the messianic era of justice and peace would have arrived.

Christians, however, believe that God has not waited for the full observance of the Torah before sending the Messiah. In fact, Christ has appeared to deliver us from the impossible task of trying to fulfill the demands of God's justice unaided. Instead, in the person of Christ, justice has at last been done, and has been seen to be done. In him the earth has witnessed a human being who perfectly embodied the justice of God, so that in his life others became the fortunate beneficiaries of God's justice, while God himself was given what was in justice his: the surrender of a free heart to his will for the world. The two — justice toward God and justice toward one's fellows — are inseparable, and both reached their consummation in the death and resurrection of Jesus.

The ascension of Jesus is perfect justice, for it means the drawing of humanity into the reign of God. It is the vindication of God's justice in the face of human injustice. It makes it possible for the whole human race in principle to find that justice which was realized in Christ. That is where Christians find themselves today: exploring the possibility of justice through surrender to God. The world cannot find justice until it is surrendered to God in Christ. When that happens, Christ will "hand over the kingdom to God the Father, having done away with every sovereignty, authority and power. . . . And when everything is subjected to him, then the Son himself will be subject in his turn to the One who subjected all things to him, so that God may be all in all" (1 Cor 15:24, 28).

In the meantime we sing the song of the Lord in an alien land. It sometimes seems naive, if not entirely inappropriate, to break bread and dream of the justice of the Kingdom in a world that takes the insanities of war, violence, and exploitation for normal. Yet, as the anonymous Christian of the second century reminds us, this is the post to which God has assigned us, and we may not lawfully desert it. In trying to remain faithful to the breaking of bread and to all that it implies, and in continuing to work, look, and pray for the coming Kingdom, Christians might take heart from the words of the Second Vatican Council:

> We can justly consider that the future of humanity
> lies in the hands of those who are strong enough
> to provide coming generations
> with reasons for living and hoping (*GS* 31).

Preaching the Just Word

WALTER J. BURGHARDT, S.J.

In MAY 1979, passions flamed in our nation's capital. Mass was about to begin in St. Matthew's Cathedral—a Mass to mark Argentina's national day. Unexpectedly, the assembled Argentinians—embassy officials, military leaders, and others—were addressed from the sanctuary by a priest-protester. For six years this missionary had ministered to a Buenos Aires shantytown; he told how he had been imprisoned and tortured, how priest friends had simply disappeared. He wanted the congregation to join him in a prayer for reconciliation. But at that moment "the organist drowned him out . . . the microphone went dead . . . the rector of the cathedral . . . told [him] to move on."[1]

The trouble seemed to be over; the forty-or-so demonstrators moved from church to street and the liturgy opened. But the preceding was only prelude. The homilist, head of the Spanish Secretariat of the archdiocese, appeared in symbolic purple. Instead of the usual eulogy, he quoted statements by John Paul II and the bishops of Latin America about repression, torture, and disappearances, about the attempt of governments to justify such activities on the basis of national security. He began to focus on the people who had vanished under the Videla regime and quoted Scripture on Herod's slaughter of the innocents.

WALTER J. BURGHARDT, S.J., a patristic scholar, is theologian-in-residence at Georgetown University and editor of *Theological Studies*. This paper was delivered at the eighth annual Notre Dame Conference on Pastoral Liturgy, June 1979.

At that juncture the congregation (three hundred or more) stormed angrily out of the church, led by a high-ranking general. Some damned the homilist for "turning a religious event into a political one." Another said "priests have no place in politics. He should have given a sermon on another subject, like the love of God."[2] But the archdiocesan director of communications said "he had no objection to the way the sermon was handled. . . . 'We hope our priests are teaching the truth,' he said. 'Whether what they say is offensive and bothers the conscience of some people should not be the issue. The issue should be whether it is the truth.'"[3]

The scene at St. Matthew's provides a stirring context for my address; perhaps it will put teeth into it. You see, the title thrust upon me is deceptive. What could be less threatening, more pacifying, than the sleepy subject "Preaching the Just Word"? In point of fact, as the Argentinian incident demonstrates, there are three "sleepers" here: the first is theological, the second liturgical, the third homiletic. The theological question: Does a Church committed to eternal salvation have anything to do with everyday justice? The liturgical question: If the Church has a role to play in the area of justice, how can this possibly affect the liturgy? The homiletic question: If justice does enter the liturgy of the worshiping community, should the preacher preach it — and if so, how?

I

My first question is theological: Does a Church committed to eternal salvation have anything to do with everyday justice? The question is basic, for unless we address that issue, there is no point in asking the next two questions: How does justice enter the liturgy? How do we preach justice?

To get concrete, should the Church speak out on economic injustice, on the fact that at this moment at least 460 million people are hungry? Should the bishops of Chile have criticized their government in 1974 "for violating human rights, creating a climate of insecurity and terror. . . ."?[4] Should Bishop Donal Lamont have castigated the Rhodesian regime for racial discrimination and repression? Should the Church take a position on the Vietnam war, on California lettuce or Farah slacks, on capital punishment or the Panama Canal, or ERA or federal aid for abortions?

I give these examples simply as examples, not to debate the merits of any of them; for these are complex issues. My question is broader than any example. Does the Church, precisely as Church, have a mission that includes justice and human rights? Does the Church have a role to play in the social, political, and economic orders?

Many Christians, many Catholics, shout a resounding no. As they see it, the Church, as Church, has *no* commission to right human injustice. The Church is a spiritual institution, and its mission is sheerly spiritual: it is a channel that links the human person with God. The Church's charge is to help us know, love, and serve God in this life and to be happy with him forever in the next. Oh yes, poverty and politics, injustice and inhumanity, may stand as barriers to God's grace. If they do, then the Church must struggle against them — but not as a direct facet of its mission, only as obstacles at the outer edge of its vocation. The Church's commission is to gather a band of true believers who will prepare themselves by faith and hope for the redemptive action by which God establishes his Kingdom at the end of history.

Two recent examples. A letter from Texas takes Msgr. George G. Higgins to task for his views on the Church and social justice. Christ "did not relieve suffering"; he simply forgave sins. In consequence, the Church should not be concerned about violations of social justice. Like Christ, it should concentrate on showing us that "it is the hardness of men's hearts that causes our suffering" and that "as long as the angel of darkness roams the world in search of souls and men fail to reject sin, human misery will continue to exist."[5]

Similarly, in a recent study titled *Christianity and the World Order,* Anglican author Edward Norman of Cambridge University argues that the essential thing religion should provide is a "sense of the ultimate worthlessness of human expectations of a better life on earth."[6] For Norman, "the teachings of the Savior clearly describe a personal rather than a social morality." By nature, Christianity is exclusively concerned with "the relationship of the soul to eternity."

Against such a privatized, me-and-Jesus religion the best of Catholic tradition cries out clearly, at times in anger. Papal encyclicals, from Leo XIII's *Rerum novarum* (on the rights and obligations of workers, employers, and the state) to John Paul II's address at Puebla and his first encyclical (*Redemptor hominis*), give the lie to such a thesis.

Oh indeed, the Christian has to avoid two extremes. On the one hand, salvation is not sheer socialization, personality development, liberation from oppressive structures, an end to poverty; it is a divinization. The Church's primary task is to see to it that the human person is refashioned in the image of Christ; short of this there is no salvation. God fulfills us by uniting us with himself. The essential liberation is freedom from the slavery that is sin. As Pius XII said in a 1956 allocution: "The goal which Christ assigns to [the Church] is strictly religious. . . . The Church must lead men and women to God, in order that they may give themselves over to him unreservedly. . . ."[7]

On the other hand, any program of evangelization is inadequate if the Church does not spend itself to free the human person from every inhuman shackle. Oh yes, the Church has good news to preach even to those whose situation is humanly hopeless; for *the* good news is Jesus — Jesus alive, yearning to make those who are heavy-burdened one with him. Sanctity is possible in poverty-ridden Appalachia, in the political prisons of the Philippines, in the excrement of Calcutta. But this does not exempt the people of God from the ceaseless struggle to transform the city of man into the Kingdom of God — a Kingdom of peace, of justice, of love.

This is the vision that emerged from the Second Vatican Council — resoundingly in its Decree on the Apostolate of the Laity:

> Christ's redemptive work, while of its nature directed to the salvation of men and women, involves also the renewal of the whole temporal order. The Church has for mission, therefore, not only to bring to men and women the message of Christ and his grace, but also to saturate and perfect the temporal sphere with the spirit of the gospel. . . . The two spheres [spiritual and temporal], distinct though they are, are so linked in the single plan of God that he himself purposes in Christ to take up the whole world again into a new creation, initially here on earth, completely on the last day.[8]

This is the vision of the 1971 Synod of Bishops in its message "On Justice in the World": the vindication of justice and participation in the process of transforming the world is "a constitutive element of the preaching of the gospel."[9] This is the vision that emerged from the 1974 Synod of Bishops in a significant statement on "Human Rights and Reconciliation." Said the bishops in common:

> Human dignity is rooted in the image and reflection of God in each of us. It is this which makes all persons essentially equal. The integral development of persons makes more clear the divine image in them. In our time the Church has grown more deeply aware of this truth; hence she believes firmly that the promotion of human rights is required by the gospel and is central to her ministry.[10]

And in 1976 the International Theological Commission (an advisory body serving the Pope), in a very carefully articulated examination of "Human Development and Christian Salvation," argued that God's grace should sharpen the conscience of Christians, should help us build a more just world, not simply by spiritual reformation, not simply by assisting individuals:

. . . for there is a kind of "injustice that assumes institutional
shape," and as long as this obtains, the situation itself calls for a
greater degree of justice and demands reforming. Our contemporaries are no longer convinced that social structures have been
predetermined by nature and therefore are "willed by God," or
that they have their origin in anonymous evolutionary laws. Consequently, the Christian must ceaselessly point out that the institutions of society originate also in the conscience of society,
and that men and women have a moral responsibility for these institutions.

We may argue how legitimate it is to speak of "institutional sin"
or of "sinful structures," since the Bible speaks of sin in the first instance in terms of an explicit, personal decision that stems from
human freedom. But it is unquestionable that by the power of sin
injury and injustice can penetrate social and political institutions.
That is why . . . even situations and structures that are unjust
have to be reformed.

Here we have a new consciousness, for in the past these responsibilities could not be perceived as distinctly as they are
now. . . .[11]

The last sentence is highly important. We Christians "have a
new consciousness. . . ." Not that the Old Testament and the
New are silent on social issues. Those who read in Scripture a
sheerly personal morality have not sung the psalms or been
burned by the prophets, have not perceived the implications of
Jesus' message.[12] And still it remains true that the Church has
grown in its awareness of what Jeremiah's "execute justice" (Jer
7:5) and the gospel of love demand. It is in line with this growth
that John Paul II confirmed contemporary magisterial teaching
in telling the Third General Assembly of the Latin American
Bishops in Puebla: "The Church has learned [in the pages of the
gospel] that its evangelizing mission has as an indispensable part
(*como parte indispensable*) action for justice and those efforts
which the development of the human person demands. . . ."[13]

II

So far, so good: the struggle for justice is an indispensable facet of the Church's mission. But the theological question leads to the liturgical question: Granted that the Church has a vital role to play in the area of justice, how can this possibly affect the liturgy?

On principle, it should. As *sacramentum fidei*, sacrament of Christian belief, liturgy has a twin function: *exprimit* and *causat*. Liturgy should give expression to the faith-experience of the Christian people, and liturgy should mold that experience.[14] All "liturgies" express experience and mold it: country music in Nashville, professional and college football, marching bands and the New York City Ballet, the Nazi goose step and the Aztec Two Step. . . . This is what expresses and evokes the joys and frustrations of a people, their anger and violence, their loves and their hates, their pent-up emotions. If we accept the thesis of first-rate liturgiologists that Christian liturgy sacramentalizes what goes on in the rest of our lives, that the liturgical journey ritualizes the human journey, two questions challenge us: (1) In point of fact, does this liturgy express the faith-experience of this people? (2) If it does, how Catholic is that expression? The dimensions of this problem, its dangers, were brought home to me in an article by Brian Wicker:

> [The liturgical] revival [among organized Christians] had a good side — in that it stimulated mature and scholarly thought about the fundamentals of Christianity and an understanding of the depths to which secularization had gone. But it had a bad side too — the side that made it possible in some places for the Christian liturgy inside the church and the fascist liturgy outside the church to coexist, or even at times to cooperate with each other. The liturgical revival was, in its origins, a conservative or even reactionary movement, liable at times to delusions of grandeur. This gave it a certain sympathy for the trappings of fascism and made the essential atheism of the latter hard to nail down. It is perhaps not surprising that those Christians most opposed to Hitler were often those least touched by the new liturgical ideas —

either intellectual protestants like Dietrich Bonhoeffer, or simple tridentine-formed peasant-Catholics like Franz Jägerstätter. Neither is it surprising that many post-fascist secular theologies of Europe and America (including those developed under Catholic auspices) have today turned away from liturgy as a source of inspiration or hope, or have even given it up as a bad job altogether.[15]

Does it frighten you that the liturgy in a Catholic cathedral is expected to coexist with, perhaps even cooperate with, the fascist liturgy that is Argentinian repression? Does it bother you that in liturgizing, ritualizing, sacramentalizing a nation's experience, we are expected to limit our symbols to love of *God*?

In his challenging book *The Eucharist and Human Liberation*,[16] Tissa Balasuriya insists that since Eucharistic worship is at the center of Christian life, the Eucharist must affirm and promote the biblical imperative of human liberation. But, he finds, almost without exception the Eucharist has been a place where the oppressor joins the oppressed with impunity; the Eucharist has been used in cooperation with, and support of, colonizing powers; even today liberating movements do not find affirmation in Eucharistic worship. Whatever the defects of the book, however utopian its hopes, it compels us to ask a crucial question: How is it possible to celebrate Eucharist if it is not expressing the real oppressions of our people, if it is not molding a faith that liberates from all enslavements?

But precisely here a work of discrimination, of discernment, is imperative. I will assume that Joseph Gelineau's thesis is valid:

> My thesis is that the celebration of the risen Christ by the assembly of believers is one of the most effective political actions that men can perform in this world — if it is true that this celebration, by contesting any power system which oppresses mankind, proclaims, stirs up and inaugurates a new order in the created world.[17]

Here "politics" is used to describe "that *exercise of power* which controls public welfare and progress."[18] But how does the liturgy influence public welfare and progress? On the face of it, few actions seem less political than liturgy. Totalitarian regimes hostile to the Church "begin by forbidding Christians any form of self-organized action in society; they then prohibit or supervise religious instruction and preaching; but in general they allow worship as inoffensive."[19] The issue is highly complex; time forces me to simplify, and to simplify is, in a sense, to falsify.

1. Paradoxically, it is not primarily by introducing political themes, by inserting an ideology, that the liturgy becomes a social force. I am not disparaging the Mass of Protest in Latin America or the Mass for Peace in the Roman Missal; I have been moved by liberating readings from Exodus and the prophets, by "prayers of the faithful" that cry to heaven for bread and justice. I mean rather that there is a serious danger in a "celebration which tries to be political but relies more on an ideology than on the paschal dynamics of the Christian mystery"; it "very soon becomes a politicized liturgy: that is, one used for specific political ends."[20] This can mean a form of manipulation at odds with the essential nature of liturgical action. The liturgy does not of itself make Christian Democrats or make for constitutional amendments; it is not a substitute for sociology, economics, or political science.

2. And yet, as George Higgins argues, "it is still the Mass which matters most — even in the temporal order."[21] But the liturgical action effects change above all by its own inner dynamic. Why? Because the temporal order can be changed only by conversion — only if men and women turn from sin and selfishness. And for Catholics the primary source of conversion is the sacrifice of the Mass, which extends through time and space the sacrifice of the Cross through which the world is transfigured. The Mass should be the liberating adventure of the whole Church, the sacrament that frees men and women from their inherited damnable concentration on themselves, looses us from our ice-cold isolation, fashions us into brothers and sisters

agonizing not only for a Church of charity but for a world of justice.

No, the Eucharistic signs and symbols do not of themselves change social, political, and economic structures; but they should change 700 million hearts and minds, grace them to admit the oppressions of which they are victims and for which they are responsible, inspire them to work with others for the coming of a kingdom characterized by justice and love.

The problem is not whether there is a link between liturgy and liberation. The problem is that we do not allow the liturgy to liberate — even to liberate us.

III

So much for the theological question, so much for the liturgical question. The struggle for justice is an indispensable facet of the Church's mission, and the liturgy should express and mold this facet of human experience. Now for the stickiest issue of all, the homiletic question: Should the preacher preach justice — and if so, how?

The more general question — *should* I preach justice? — ought not detain us, much less paralyze us. The specific function of the homily, Yves Congar has pointed out, is not only to explain the liturgical mystery but to bring the faithful into the mystery "by throwing light on their life so that they can unite it to this mystery. When this happens, the sermon is truly a word which prompts a response."[22] You see, the liturgy's insights "are more or less veiled";[23] liturgical texts and forms tend to be immobilized, with rare exceptions are the same for all, whatever their condition. The homily extends the immemorial symbols to a particular time and place, a particular people.[24] And so I must speak to this people's needs, this people's hungers. If they need to act justly or if they hunger for justice, a liturgy that expresses and molds their faith-experience forbids me to keep silent. To say nothing is to say something.

But what do I say? How concrete dare I get? For some, the priest simply preaches the gospel, the word of God, teaches what Jesus taught. Preach the word of God and parishioners will make the right decisions in the moral order. In a word, limit yourself to general principles.

I'm afraid it will not wash, for at least two good reasons. First, it betrays a glorious tradition in the Church. It forgets how Ambrose of Milan, ordered by the Empress Justina to surrender a basilica to the Arians, *preached* a resounding no: "I am commanded," he declared to Justina's son, the Emperor Valentinian, "'Hand over the basilica!' I reply: 'It is not right for me to hand it over; nor will it profit you, Emperor, to receive it. You cannot legally violate the home of a private citizen; do you think you can take away the house of God? . . . You may not have it. . . .'"[25] It forgets that John Chrysostom, royally hated by the Empress Eudoxia, opened his homily on the feast of John the Baptist by crying: "Again Herodias raves; again she rages; again she dances; again she asks for the head of John upon a charger."[26] It will not square with John Paul II's homily in Santo Domingo on January 25, 1979:

> Making this world more just means, among other things, . . .
> to strive to have a world in which no more children lack sufficient
> nutrition, education, instruction; . . . that there be no more poor
> peasants without land . . . no more workers mistreated . . . no
> more systems which permit the exploitation of man by man or by
> the state . . . no more who have too much while others are lack-
> ing everything through no fault of their own . . . no injustice or
> inequality in administering justice; . . . that the law support
> everyone equally; that force not prevail over truth and rights
> . . . and that the economic and political never prevail over the
> human.[27]

At the beginning of his journey to Latin America, John Paul was not mouthing pious abstractions; he was addressing actual life-and-death issues.

Second, homilies that avoid concrete applications risk saying nothing. The Old Testament and the New are indeed our Bible, the privileged source of our faith and our morality. But if I mount the pulpit with "Scripture alone" in my hands, if I limit my preaching to the broad biblical imperatives, if I simply repeat scriptural slogans like "Man does not live on bread alone," "My peace I give to you," "Seek first the kingdom of God," "Love your neighbor as you love yourself," "Wives, be subject to your husbands," hungry stomachs will stay bloated, the arms race will escalate, dissidents will rot in political prisons, blacks will return to their slavery, and women will continue to be second-class citizens in much of the world. After all, it is not only the heathen who are responsible for oppression; the oppressors, large and small, often break Eucharistic bread with us. In fact, who among us is not, by act or silence, an oppressor of our brothers and sisters?

No, the gospel must be touched to concrete human living. And remember, the Church grows — the whole Church, pope as well as peasant — in its understanding of what the gospel demands. For example, in its efforts to construct a livable, viable social order, the Church has consistently stressed three facets of human living: truth, justice, and love. Only within recent times have these principles of social order been finally rounded out with a fourth principle indispensable in our days. I mean freedom. It is the growing realization that truth, justice, and love are not enough, are not really there, if the man and woman they serve are not free.

It is this that must be preached — our fresh understanding of what the perennial gospel demands or suggests in the context of our time and space. The magisterium does it (see *Mater et magistra* and *Populorum progressio*); the institutional Church need not, should not, and does not regard itself, in Karl Rahner's words, "solely as the doctrinaire guardian and teacher of abstract principles which become ever increasingly abstract and are liable to carry within themselves the danger of a terrifying sterility. . . ."[28] The Church has and should have the courage for concrete imperatives, concrete directives, "even in regard to socio-political action by Christians in the world."[29] This same courage the preacher must carry to his pulpit.

But the neuralgic problem remains: How concrete dare I get? There is no simple solution, no all-purpose push button to activate the answer. Each issue calls for blood, sweat, and tears.

At times the issue is clear. In 1964 I simply had to endorse the Civil Rights Act; there was no alternative, save the enslavement of a race. But few political and socioeconomic issues are that clear-cut. Once you get beyond the general principles — the right to live and eat and work, the right to education and health care, the right to decent housing — it is difficult to locate the evil, to identify the villain, to pinpoint the solution. I can indeed proclaim from the pulpit today what the United Nations World Food Conference proclaimed from Rome in 1974: "Every man, woman, and child has the inalienable right to freedom from hunger and malnutrition. . . ." But the causes are confoundingly complex. Is nature the villain — "acts of God"? Is it people — the world growing too fast? Is it productivity — lack of agricultural know-how? Is it our international economic order — a whole web of unjust relationships between rich and poor countries?[30] Experts, men and women of good will, disagree.

But disagreement need not strike me dumb. It can only render me mute if I see the pulpit as the podium for eternal verities alone, defined dogma, the *ipsissima verba* of Jesus. Beyond that, our delicate, indispensable task is to help form Christian consciences — not force them, form them. *Help form Christian consciences* — this is the crucial phrase, with each word of high significance. I am not an expert on world hunger and defense budgets, but without playing partisan politics I can at least wax as indignant as World Bank President Robert S. McNamara when he denounces an arms race that costs the nations more than 400 billion dollars a year, while over a billion men, women, and children live in inhuman degradation, condemned to stunted bodies, darkened minds, shortened lives.[31] I do not know the political solution; I cannot fashion a budget; but I do know that those horrifying figures add up to a moral evil. Given that moral evil, how can I fail to echo the cry of HEW Secretary Joseph A. Califano, Jr., at Notre Dame's commencement: "Of all the judgments of history and God we should fear, it is their judgment on our continued failure to use the means at hand to end the hunger of the world that we should fear most"?[32] This much at the very least God's people can expect of me: in the midst of my mind's chaos, a cry from the heart.

But what if I am convinced I do have the answer? The answer to the arms race is unilateral disarmament; to abortion, a constitutional amendment; to the parochial-school crisis, tax credits; to capital punishment, life imprisonment; to feminine enslavement, the ERA; to migrant-worker injustice, a boycott of grapes and lettuce; to Rhodesia, economic sanctions. These are indeed moral issues, but may I preach my own solution in the name of the gospel? Of all homiletic minefields, this may well be the most perilous. I shall move quickly and warily, aware that each step could trigger an explosion.

1. I do not see how you can bar the controversial from the pulpit simply because it is controversial. After all, I cannot be content with glittering generalities; I must move the gospel to this age, to this people; but the meaning and demands of the gospel today are chock-full of complexity. And the more complex an issue, the more open to controversy.

2. With Peter Henriot and George Higgins, I submit that "the pulpit, as a general rule, is not the proper forum in which to pontificate on complicated and highly controversial political and socio-economic issues."[33] Here the crucial word is "pontificate." On such issues, in a short span of time, with no room for counterargument, I dare not speak in dogmatic fashion, as if I alone am the trumpet of the Lord.

3. If I dare not dogmatize, I may still raise the issues, lay them out, even tell the people where I stand and why — not to impose my convictions as gospel, but to quicken their Christian conscience, to spur them to personal reflection.

4. I may not take unfair advantage of a captive audience, especially since the expertise in the pews often exceeds my own. Inasmuch as the suffering faithful, however sorely provoked, are expected by immemorial custom to hold their tongues as I empty my quiver against the ERA, I should provide another forum — parish hall, smaller discussion groups — where controversial issues may be properly debated, where all who wish to speak their piece may be heard. I must guard against a persistent priestly peril, where I see the ordained minister as alone bearing the burden of Christian guidance and pastoral counseling. No, all of us are in this together; all of us, pope included, belong to an *ecclesia discens,* a Church that is learning.

5. In line with that realization — we are one body, animated by the same Spirit, and all of us need one another — many a priest must reappraise his attitude toward the people who must listen to him. Some years ago an Irish layman rapped our homiletic knuckles sharply:

> I am afraid that too often our preachers entirely ignore what we, the silent faithful, expect to hear in a sermon. . . . They address us as rebels whom they must subdue; as idlers whom they must shake up; as hardened sinners whom they must needs terrify; as the proud who require to be humiliated; as the self-satisfied who need to be disquieted. . . . [They] are never done telling us of our duties and of our neglect of duty. . . . But if you come to examine it, there is really nothing easier than to put forward a person's duty; and to hand out reproaches costs nothing either. . . . The thing which is really difficult, which is actually divine, is to give us a taste for our duties, and to awaken in us a wish to do them and to be generous in the doing. And another name for a taste for duty is love. Beloved preachers, then, make us love God, or rather, help us to believe in his love for us.[34]

Those striking words troubled me from the moment I discovered them, especially the last several sentences: the divine thing "is to give us a taste for our duties . . . . help us to believe in [God's] love for us." Unexpectedly, that entreaty brought me back from the homily proper to the broader liturgy, from the homilist homilizing to the celebrant celebrating. For in this context of the just word, a Jesuit colleague at the Woodstock Theological Center in Washington, John C. Haughey, recaptured for me a remarkable insight expressed by government people engaged in a Woodstock project on government decision-making. As they saw it, good liturgy facilitates public responsibility not because it provides principles of solution, not because it tells the people what precisely to think about specific conflicts, but rather because a celebrant who effectively celebrates the transcendent puts them in touch with that which transcends all their burning concerns, their particular perplexities. Good liturgy frees them to sort out the issues they have to decide, because it makes them aware of their addictions and their illusions, casts a pitiless light on myopic self-interest, detaches from a narrow selfishness, facilitates Christian discernment. In that sense liturgy is not so much didactic as evocative. Let *God* transpire; let *God* speak.

A distressing question has taken hold of me and will not leave me: Is it possible that in my understandable yearning to link liturgizing to justice and human rights, I have been saying too much and celebrating too little?

A final word. It has to do with a principle I stressed some years ago at the Notre Dame Pastoral Liturgy Conference: Ultimately, *I* am the word, the word that is heard.[35] Ralph Waldo Emerson insisted that "the preacher should be a poet." He meant that "a man's sermon should be rammed with life."[36] That is why, in the midst of a famous iconoclastic address at the Harvard Divinity School on July 15, 1838, he railed at the junior pastor of his grandfather Ripley's church in Concord:

> I once heard a preacher who sorely tempted me to say I would go to church no more. . . . He had lived in vain. He had no one word intimating that he had laughed or wept, was married or in love, had been commended, or cheated, or chagrined. If he had ever lived or acted, we were none the wiser for it. The capital secret of his profession, namely, to convert life into truth, he had

not learned. Not one fact in all his experience, had he yet imported into his doctrine. . . . Not a line did he draw out of real history. The true preacher can always be known by this, that he deals out to the people his life, — life passed through the fire of thought.[37]

It is understandable that our people hear no word from us intimating that we are married or "in love." It passes understanding that our people rarely sense from the homiletic word that our hearts are in anguish because Christians are murdering Christians in Northern Ireland, because ten million Americans go to bed hungry each night, because human rights are bloodied in South Africa, because two hundred thousand homeless humans have to defecate at curbstones in Calcutta, because on my street there are people who are lonely or hungry or scared. Can they feel that I get angry, that I cry, that I beat my fists against a wall in frustration, that I shout out to God against his own seeming injustice? Or do they feel that in my case "the just word" is just a word and nothing more?

At this point I am speechless. After three months of relentless research and reflection, after mountains of paper and a million words, after fifty-six minutes of close reasoning and impassioned argument, what I put to you most urgently on preaching the just word goes beyond the word that is preached. I phrase it in two questions. (1) Do you *live* the just word you preach? Are you, as St. James puts it, a "doer" of the just word, "a doer that acts" (Jas 1:22-25), or do you simply speak it? Does your just word leap forth from some experience of our sorry human condition? Is it your life that passes through the fire of your thought? (2) How do you *celebrate* the just word, the Word who *is* Justice? Do the faithful sense that it is *your* body too that is being offered for them, *your* blood too that is being shed for them? From your celebration of transcendence, do they experience the God who enables them to "execute justice"?

The Sacrifice of Thanksgiving
And Social Justice

EDWARD J. KILMARTIN, S.J.

IN THE LITURGY of the Mass, the community gathers together to consecrate itself to the service of the Father in communion with its Lord Jesus Christ through the Holy Spirit. This is what the great Eucharistic liturgies of the East and West affirm. It is, therefore, altogether fitting that the community's concern for social justice be explicitly articulated in both the Liturgy of the Word and the Liturgy of the Eucharist, through the homily and fixed prayers. It is also proper that the community's commitment to social justice be symbolically actualized in such a way that its relation to worship of the Father is unmistakable. In other words, the connection between worship and social action in the world should be experienced in the word and act of the liturgy.

This thesis can be developed in several ways. Within the scope of this essay, it is treated from the viewpoint of the Roman Catholic theology of the Mass. A brief discussion of the link between the "holy sacrifice" of the Mass and the whole life of believers is followed by a systematic presentation of the relationship between the Mass and social justice. For the sake of con-

EDWARD J. KILMARTIN, S.J., is professor of liturgy at the University of Notre Dame. He is the author of *The Eucharist in the Primitive Church* and has contributed to numerous scholarly publications, particularly in the area of sacramental and liturgical theology.

venience, relevant texts of the Second Vatican Council are used
to formulate the basic position of Roman Catholic theology on
this issue. Finally, the question of the concrete application of this
theology to liturgical practice, the main concern of this essay, is
raised. One aspect of this problem is offered for consideration:
the symbolism of the collections that are made in the context of
the liturgy of the Mass.

In this latter connection, the lesson of history is introduced. In
the early Church, material offerings were an expression of the
relation between liturgy and social justice. In the course of time,
however — and here the discussion is confined to the Western
tradition — they became more related to personal concerns for
salvation. An understanding of this development and the underlying causes may provide an important contribution to the
resolution of a liturgical problem that deserves some attention.
From it we can, perhaps, gain some clues to help us in the for-
mulation of an approach to this question: How can the collections at the Mass become once again an expression of social concern and so contribute to heightening Christian awareness of the
obligation of justice and love in daily life?

I. The Holy Sacrifice

The Christ who meets the believer in the heart of the liturgy is
the Holy One, the Consecrated One, who invites Christians,
made holy through baptism, to continually reconsecrate themselves to the Father in the power of the Spirit. The fullness of this
teaching is expressed in the pregnant saying of Paul: "All is
yours, and you are Christ's, and Christ is God's" (1 Cor 3:22).
We can only outline some features of this theme that are immediately relevant to our topic.

Religion expresses itself in the scope of ethics. But there is a
danger that the religious act will be deprived of substance if one
forgets that the highest virtue and truly perfect act of love consists in the complete surrender to God of one's whole being and

in placing one's possessions at his disposal. From this point of view, nothing is profane; everything belongs to the Father, the creator of all, and must be reconsecrated to him. This is what the Father claims and his presence demands.

In the Mass, the memorial of the death and resurrection of Jesus Christ, the consecration of Christ and of the community in Christ to the Father is proclaimed through the great prayer of praise and thanksgiving. This solemn celebration of the faith makes an explicit claim on the participants to include the whole of their lives in this consecration. This claim is not always honored. The holy sacrifice can be betrayed; it can be handed over to the realm of empty ritualism without a vital bond to the whole of one's life. This happens when the commitment to love the Father as son or daughter, expressed with the lips, does not include a real commitment to love all humankind as brothers and sisters of the same Father both in intention and in concrete action.

II. The Mass and Social Justice

The theme of social justice receives some attention in the Pastoral Constitution on the Church in the Modern World (*Gaudium et spes*) of the Second Vatican Council. We read in this text what modern Catholic theologians have been emphasizing: The equal dignity of human beings, in virtue of their divine calling and destiny, demands that excessive economic and social disparity between individuals and peoples be eradicated (*GS* 29).[1] Consequently, the plea is made that Catholics strive to transcend merely individualistic morality, and the advice is given: "The best way to fulfill one's obligations of justice and love is to contribute to the common good according to one's means and the needs of others . . . ." (*GS* 30).[2]

The Constitution goes on to single out the Church as the place where human solidarity is especially manifested. Christ is said to have established, by the gift of the Spirit, "a new brotherly communion among all who received him in faith and love; this is the communion of his own body, the Church, in which everyone as members one of the other would render mutual service in the measure of the different gifts bestowed on each" (GS 32).[3] Hence the obligation of the Church to work for the realization of social justice is acknowledged (GS 41–43).[4]

A frequently quoted statement of the Dogmatic Constitution on the Church (Lumen gentium) also points in this direction: ". . . the Church, in Christ, is in the nature of sacrament – a sign and instrument, that is, of communion with God and of unity among all men" (LG 1).[5] This understanding of the Church certainly implies that it has the mission to work for the realization of social justice. But how is this mission related to the Mass?

Drawing on modern Eucharistic theology, which stresses the relation of the Eucharist to the Church, Lumen gentium states: "Taking part in the eucharistic sacrifice, the source and summit of the Christian life, [the faithful] offer the divine victim to God and themselves along with it" (LG 11).[6] The official commentary on this text, found in the Instruction on the Worship of the Eucharistic Mystery (May 25, 1967), explains it as follows:

> The Eucharist both perfectly signifies and wonderfully effects that sharing in God's life and unity of God's people by which the Church exists. It is the summit of both the action by which God sanctifies the world in Christ, and the worship which men offer to Christ and which through him they offer to the Father in the Spirit. Its celebration "is the supreme means by which the faithful come to express in their lives and to manifest to others the mystery of Christ and the true nature of the Church."[7]

Given this understanding, it follows that the mission of the Church to work for social justice should be manifested and realized in the celebration of the Eucharist. But how is this to be done in the concrete? Here we can treat only one aspect of the problem: the function of the liturgical collections.

III. THE LESSON OF HISTORY

During the formative period of the Christian Church, up to the third century, the celebration of the Lord's Supper was called "Eucharist." This reflected the common understanding that the assembly's act is best characterized as one of thanksgiving to the Father in the memorial of the death and resurrection of Jesus Christ. Communion with the risen Lord and union of the participants with one another were expressed and deepened through the sharing of the holy bread and cup. The bread and wine, too, were called Eucharist, because they became the sacrament of the Body and Blood of Jesus Christ through the response of the Word of God to the word of the community's prayer of thanksgiving proclaimed through its leader.[8]

All the participants were considered to have an active role in this sacrifice of thanksgiving. This was expressed by the response "Amen" to the prayer of thanksgiving made by the chief celebrant. Corresponding to this, the bringing of the bread and wine for the liturgy, as well as contributions made for the needy, was an expression of membership in the new People of God. No special reward for the individual donors was expected; rather, the social meaning was predominant.

At the outset of the third century, in North Africa, an intimate relation was seen between the presentation of bread and wine by the faithful and the central act of the Lord's Supper. This presentation was considered symbolic of their co-offering of the Eucharist with the chief celebrant. Since the dead were regarded as members of the Church, it was natural that they should be drawn into the fellowship of the earthly worshipers by gifts offered "in their name."[9]

There is also evidence that other material gifts besides bread and wine were offered by the faithful. These, too, were called "sacrificial gifts" for God.[10] Expressive of thanksgiving to God and of the solidarity of the community, they were taken from the altar and given to God's needy.

A different approach to the relationship between the laity and their gifts and the Eucharistic sacrifice is taken in the *Didascalia*, a Church order originating in North Syria about 240 A.D. The roles of the bishop and the laity are described in terms of the Old Testament model of priesthood and sacrifice. The gifts presented by the laity are not considered as symbols of their co-offering; rather, they are sacrifices of almsgiving that are commended to God by the bishop as mediator of the community along the lines of the Old Testament priest.[11] The beginnings of a different evaluation of the presentation of the gifts peculiar to the East, in contrast to that of North Africa and Rome, are already evident.

So far we have seen verified a principle that continues to be applicable down to the present day: The meaning attached to the presentation of gifts at the Eucharist is determined by the basic idea that governs the understanding of the Eucharist in any given period. In the first three centuries, the Eucharist was seen as a celebration of praise and thanksgiving. Consequently, where this view was not substantially modified by the introduction of the Old Testament theology of priesthood and sacrifice, the gifts were regarded simply as a thank-offering to God.

In keeping with the high value set on alms in both the Old and New Testaments, contributions for the poor were considered by Christians to evoke a favorable response from God. This concept was attached to the liturgical offerings in the *Didascalia*, as the understanding of the Eucharistic sacrifice became influenced by the Old Testament theology of priesthood and sacrifice.[12] Otherwise, and more generally, the material gifts were not given in the Eucharist precisely to obtain God's favor. They expressed one's membership in the worshiping community and were regarded as a thank-offering to God. As such, they were taken from the altar to serve God's poor, including, in increasing measure, the clergy, who were beginning to live solely from the support of the Church.

As long as the Lord's Supper is understood simply as the Eucharist of the community, the place where believers manifest and realize themselves as the community of the new People of God through prayer and acts of thanksgiving, the explicit question about the reward that accrues from the presentation of gifts is not considered. Thus, for example, we find no discussion at the outset of the third century in North Africa about the meaning for salvation of the offerings "for the dead." They are understood as the expression of the fellowship of the living and dead, symbolic of the co-offering of the Eucharist by the dead with the living.[13]

For our purposes here, the subsequent developments in the East need not concern us except insofar as they influenced Western practice. We may, therefore, now turn to the changes related to the offering of gifts that took place in the West beginning in the latter part of the third century.

At the outset of this period, we find evidence of a growing persuasion that the Eucharist is a privileged place where personal concerns obtain a special hearing before God. This is reflected in the addition of names and petitions in the liturgical prayer. The names of offerers are mentioned along with intercessions for individual concerns.[14] Thus, in the fourth and fifth centuries, the old North African and Roman offertory procession is considered not only as a way of expressing active participation in the Eucharistic sacrifice but also as a means of obtaining something for oneself through inclusion by remembrance or petition. Otherwise in the West, where the offertory procession was not practiced, gifts were brought and offered in a variety of ways as "spiritual sacrifices" in their own right, and the donors were named in the liturgy. The Gallican liturgy, influenced by Eastern practices, provides one example of this.[15]

In the further development of the theology of the Eucharist in the West, from the sixth to the ninth century the Eucharistic sacrifice came to be considered everywhere as a unified act accomplished by the priest as representative of the people and as a significant means of obtaining certain favors for the living and the dead.[16] The older Roman concept of the Eucharist as a series of differentiated activities of the priest and people, which, taken together, symbolize the active co-offering of the whole community, no longer provided the basic idea governing the understanding of the liturgical act. As might be expected, traces of the older North African and Roman view persisted in the West even beyond this period. The accent, though, was decidedly on the role of the priest as mediator.[17]

Seen as a unified act accomplished by the priest, the Mass was offered upon request. Gifts were given with a view to a special remembrance by the celebrant of the liturgy. During the seventh and eighth centuries, the gift was not considered to obligate the priest in a special way even if each donor expected to be named in the great petition. However, a new development occurred among the German peoples at this time. Gradually a recompense came to be expected for a gift given to the church or the priest. This custom had its roots in German law, in which it belonged to the essence of a gift to be sealed by a recompense.[18] The church or priest was expected to provide in some way for the care of the soul of the donor and his or her intentions. At first, mention in the prayer of petition was considered to be a fitting remuneration, but by the end of the eighth century, Masses were brought into the sphere of ecclesiastical recompense.[19]

At the end of the early Middle Ages, the elements of a new theological synthesis were already present and partially integrated in the whole Western Church. This had a profound effect on the practice of offering gifts (by this time usually money) in connection with the celebration of a Mass and on the understanding of the relation of the gifts to the Mass. This theological synthesis developed over the eleventh and twelfth centuries and reached its term in the thirteenth century.

The old offertory procession of the Roman liturgy kept alive the concept of the co-offering of the people. It provided the impetus for a varied system of offerings in which the individual could entrust his or her gift to the priest and so be inserted by him into the Eucharistic sacrifice even if the gift was not personally presented at the liturgy. Even if absent, he or she could share in the blessing of the sacrifice through the priest who accepted his or her intention and made it his own.

The concept of the Eucharist behind this practice derived from the merging of different spheres of law; Old Testament, German, and Roman legal elements mutually determined the role of priest and people in the Mass.[20] In addition, new developments in the theology of the Eucharist, extending over the period from the ninth to the thirteenth century, increasingly promoted the idea that the priest alone is active in the celebration.

As we have already seen, German law provided the concept of recompense for a gift. The fitting remuneration for a gift to the church or priest was mention in the prayer of petition or Masses. The Old Testament, which contains much legal material on worship and priesthood, provided the legal basis for presenting a gift to the priest who acted as mediator. Through him, as in the case of the Old Testament priests, the donor became offerer. With the upswing of the theological sciences in the early Scholastic period, Roman law played a significant role in many ways.[21] The Scholastic attempt to determine scientifically what can be expected from a Mass by the offerer of a gift was clearly influenced by the demands of this law for a clear comprehension and description of legally significant proceedings and relations.

Through the integration of the Roman, German, and Old Testament concepts, the donor of a gift was seen both as inducing the priest to offer a Mass for a definite request and, at the same time, as acting in the role of a member of the worshiping community alongside the priest who accepted the gift. He or she had an intimate share in the fruits of the Eucharistic sacrifice as soon as the gift was related to it by the priest.

Old Testament, German, and Roman law contributed immensely to the sharpening of the distinction between the roles of priest and people in the celebration of the Mass. The cooperation of the people was expressed by their requests for Masses. The priest was said to offer "for the people," and the people were described as offering "through the hands of the priest." But the priest was seen primarily as the representative of the people insofar as he was their mediator, after the model of the Old Testament priest. Hence he was generally regarded as the sole acting subject. [22]

The sharp distinction between the activities of priest and people was further heightened by the consequences of the theological debate that began in earnest in the ninth century. [23] Two concepts of the Eucharist had been inherited from the past. One stressed the role of the Eucharist in building up the Church. In contrast to this Augustinian point of view, another one, which derived from the East and found its way into the Gallican liturgy, focused on the consecration of the elements and their relation to the risen Lord. In the course of this debate, the emphasis was firmly placed on the Real Presence of Christ under the forms of bread and wine and the decisive role the priest plays in pronouncing the *verba Domini,* that is, the words of Jesus in the account of the institution of the Eucharist. This further accentuated the separation of the activity of the priest from that of the laity in the Mass.

Moreover, the debate about the relationship of the signs to the mystery of Christ's presence resulted in dividing the Eucharistic mystery into (1) the sacrament of the Real Presence; (2) the sacrificial action. The breakdown of the ancient concept of sacrament, according to which the Church's ritual activity and symbols contain the mystery that they signify, occurred in the conceptual world of the German peoples. [24] It precipitated the debate on the Real Presence of the risen Lord under the forms of bread and wine. This debate was settled by the appeal to the words of Christ spoken at the Last Supper and the patristic tradition that speaks of the change of bread and wine into the Body and Blood of Christ. Further support for this sacramental realism was afforded by the development of the doctrine of transubstantiation.

But in the sphere of the theology of the sacrifice of the Mass, the breakdown of the old concept of sacrament was fully carried through. Medieval theology took for granted that the sacrifice of the Cross is unrepeatable, that is, it is historically finished. Hence it was assumed that the truth of this sacrifice lies outside the ritual repetition that occurs in the Mass.[25] Consequently, the symbolic action of the Mass was reduced almost to a graphic representation of the past sufferings of Christ, which, together with the sacramental signs of his Real Presence, was calculated to awaken in the believers the remembrance of the Passion and to bestow the fruits of the past redemptive action.

From this point of view, the Mass appeared as a sacrifice somehow added to that of the Cross. To be sure, it was linked to the Cross through the presence of the Victim of the Cross under the symbols of his Passion and because the fruits of the Cross are distributed through the Mass. But the concept of the active presence of Christ offering the sacrifice of the Cross in, with, and through the community was lacking. Rather, the sacrifice of the Cross and the Mass were incorrectly conjoined through the role of the priest, who was understood to act as the representative of Christ. He had the "power over the Body of Christ" to bring about the sacramental presence as instrument of Christ and also to offer the sacrifice of the Mass in Christ's name as well as in the name of the Church.

This understanding of the Mass explains in part the medieval preaching about the sacrifice of the Cross being offered for original sin and the Mass for daily sins, as well as the expanded teaching about the various fruits of the Mass. This preaching and teaching served to remedy to some extent the emptying of the mystery content of Christ's active offering of his sacrifice in the Mass. Since the priest was seen as the representative of Christ and of the Church in the Mass, he naturally came to be awarded the function of distributing the blessings derived from the re-presentation of the one, unique sacrifice of the Cross. On the other hand, as the representative of the Church, the priest was likewise assigned the role of distributing the blessings derived from the devotion of the Church expressed in the Mass. The blessings derived from the Mass as the re-presentation of the sacrifice of the Cross were considered unlimited in themselves because of their source: the Cross of Christ. However, they were interpreted in various ways as limited in their application to the individual recipient.[26] The blessings derived from the Mass as sacrifice of the Church were seen as limited because of the always imperfect devotion of the Church on earth.[27]

This concept of limited fruits of the Mass implied that one could gain more from a Mass offered exclusively for one's intention. Initially in the German sphere, when a gift was given to oblige the priest to offer Mass for a particular intention, this did not prevent him from accepting other gifts and applying the intention of the donors to the same Mass. Already in the ninth century, however, the practice of offering Mass for one intention to the exclusion of others had gained a foothold in German circles.[28] It seems that the concept of the Mass as a unified sacrificial act implanted the idea that one could benefit more if it were offered exclusively for one intention. This practice was resisted by the Roman Church and its theologians for the next three centuries,[29] but in the thirteenth century the practice also prevailed in the Roman Church and was made the basis for the theological conclusion that the fruits derived from each Mass are limited before application. From this reasoning was formulated the canonical rule that forms the basis of the traditional Western explanation of the Mass stipend: the priest who accepts a gift for a Mass is obliged to offer it for the intention of one donor to the exclusion of others.[30]

Through the development we have described, the Mass came to be considered as an objective instrument of blessings under the control of the priest. In virtue of his intention, which is not a petition but an act of his will, he distributes shares in the blessings of the Eucharistic sacrifice. His power over the Mass includes his power to determine for whom he will offer it.

IV. MODERN INTERPRETATIONS OF LITURGICAL OFFERINGS

From the thirteenth to the twentieth century, the Mass stipend has been the traditional means by which the faithful are linked to the Eucharistic sacrifice in a special way. But this offering "for a Mass" was not conceived as a symbolic way of expressing the active co-offering of the faithful with the priest. It was understood, not as an expression of the consecration of the fruits of one's labor in connection with the worship of God, but as a means of obtaining special consideration from the priest. It served as a request for a Mass and as a contribution to the support of the priest acting on behalf of the donor.

Other gifts presented at the liturgy for the support of the Church and the poor were given no special religious meaning or were seen either as the fulfillment of the obligation to support the Church or as a sacrifice of almsgiving. In any case, they were not generally interpreted as symbolic of the consecration of the fruits of one's work to God in and through the active co-offering of the Eucharistic sacrifice with the priest.

Today, however, reflection on the significance of the Mass stipend has led Catholic theologians to interpret it as an expression of the devotion of the donor and thus symbolic of one's integration into the worship of the Mass.[31] Pope Paul VI, in his instruction on Mass stipends, *Firma in traditione* (June 15, 1974), interprets the stipend as a sacrifice of almsgiving by which the faithful more intimately associate themselves with Christ offering himself as victim and as an expression of their fellowship with the priest who exercises his ministry on their behalf.[32]

While agreeing that the stipend should be given a religious meaning as a form of integration into the Mass, Catholic theologians debate about the relation between the stipend and the old Roman offertory procession. In the theology underlying the Roman offertory procession, the priest represents the faithful in the celebration. The people offer the sacrifice through him as their representative, but actively. In this conception of the

Eucharist, stress is placed on the individual prayers and actions that are gathered by the priest as chief celebrant to form one meaning.

This view is in sharp contrast to that of the Catholic theology of the Middle Ages, which interpreted the Eucharist as a unified sacrificial act accomplished by the priest independently of, and at the same time in the name of, the people. This interpretation continues to influence Catholic theology today. A variation of it is found in Pius XII's encyclical *Mediator Dei*. Here we read that the priest, as representative of Christ, performs the unbloody immolation at the words of consecration. Therefore, as representative of Christ, he offers Christ at the level of the rite of consecration of the gifts. He does not represent the faithful in this action. The encyclical states, however, that the faithful can be said to offer the sacrifice at this moment "by the hands of the priest." This is so because the priest represents Christ, the head of the Mystical Body, who offers the sacrifice in the name of the Church. On the other hand, the faithful are described as offering with the priest, who acts as their representative by uniting their prayers with his prayer. Hence, the active part that the faithful play in the Eucharistic sacrifice is affirmed (*MD* 92–93).[33]

Vatican II's Dogmatic Constitution on the Church repeats this teaching: "in the person of Christ [the priest] effects the eucharistic sacrifice and offers it to God in the name of all the people. The faithful indeed, by virtue of their royal priesthood, participate in the offering of the Eucharist" (*LG* 10).[34] Pope Paul VI also employs this theology in *Firma in traditione* when he teaches that the primary goal of the offering of a stipend is to unite the donor "more closely with Christ offering himself as a victim," and when he says that the faithful "add to it [the Eucharistic sacrifice] a form of sacrifice of their own."[35]

The foregoing official documents agree with the concept of the Eucharist as a unified sacrificial act effected by the priest as direct representative of Christ, independently of his function to represent the people in their active role. Yet, these official writings do accept an important aspect of the theology behind the old Roman offertory procession: while not embracing the theological understanding of the inner relationship between the roles of priest and people that it expresses, these documents do emphasize the active role of the laity.

Some modern liturgists and theologians go a step further in favor of the theological perspective of the old Roman offertory procession.[36] It can be argued that the priest is representative of the faith of the Church at the level of the whole rite of the Mass. His activity, therefore, connotes the active presence of Christ, the head of the Church, who, with the Spirit, is the ultimate source of the act of faith of the worshiping community.

From this point of view, the priest represents Christ by representing the Church and, at the same time, represents the Church by representing Christ. This reciprocal relation is possible because the priest directly represents the Eucharistic faith of the community and so acts in the person of Christ, who, together with the Spirit, is the grounds for the acceptable act of sacrificial praise and thanksgiving made by the Church. Consequently, the offertory procession may be viewed as a symbolic expression of the integration of the offerers into the prayer of praise that the priest pronounces in the name of all. It signifies the real co-offering of the participants, who perform the visible liturgical rite in and with the priest who directly represents them.

Accordingly, the stipend cannot be interpreted simply as a sacrifice of almsgiving "added to the Eucharistic sacrifice." For the Eucharist is not seen as containing a unified sacrificial act accomplished by the priest independently of, and at the same time in the name of, the people, that is, the rite of the "unbloody immolation" that takes place at the moment when the "words of consecration" are spoken. Rather, the Eucharist is understood as a constellation of prayers and actions forming one unified meaning: the consecration of the community of believers in, with, and through Christ. The stipend, therefore, is seen as contributing to the constitution of the one visible liturgical rite.

At present, the relative value of these different theological approaches to the Mass stipend is under discussion. Nevertheless, Catholic theologians are in agreement that the proper meaning of the stipend does not lie in the material sphere; it is not merely a means of providing for the support of the clergy. Pope Paul VI affirms that it is primarily a way of participation in the sacrifice and secondarily a means of support for the priest.[37]

But perhaps we should see the stipend more in terms of the needs of the Church, with reference to its secondary meaning. This would bring the stipend closer to the traditional meaning of the collections, which were not intended exclusively for the support of the clergy. Perhaps, also, the meaning of the stipend as an expression of sacrificial devotion should be extended to all collections made in the liturgy of the Eucharist.

The interpretation of collections in this way, which renders obsolete the practice of the Mass stipend, finds support in Paul VI's *Firma in traditione.* Here he describes the significance of offerings in the early Church: "It is a long-established tradition in the Church that the faithful, desiring in a religious and ecclesial spirit to participate more intimately in the Eucharistic Sacrifice, add to it a form of sacrifice of their own by which they contribute in a particular way to the needs of the Church and especially to the sustenance of its ministers."[38]

Inserted into the memorial of the sacrifice of Christ, the offering of gifts should be an expression of thanksgiving to God, a consecration of the material world and human work to God. At the same time, it becomes an expression of the truth that true service of God always involves the service of humankind. These gifts build up the Church in the measure that the donor and the priest, who receives them from the altar, make use of them to express a priestly vocation. Through the gifts the donor expresses his or her priestly service of God and God's poor; the priest who receives them from the altar should distribute them to God's poor. In this way both the donor and priest answer the summons of the gospel to live the whole of life as a cultic act.

V. SUMMARY

1. The basic idea governing the understanding of the Lord's Supper determines the interpretation of the gifts presented at the liturgy. In the first three centuries, the Eucharist was understood as a sacrifice of thanksgiving by which the participants expressed their membership in the new People of God. The gifts symbolized gratitude for the blessings of the new covenant relationship between God and humankind. As such, they were freely given in the liturgy "before God" without thought of recompense and bestowed on God's poor in fulfillment of the social obligations of the new covenant.

In the following centuries in the West, paralleling the gradual identification of clergy with the Church and of the laity with the world, the sacral sphere of the liturgy became understood as the almost exclusive domain of the priest. The laity lost confidence in their ability to stand before God in the Mass. It was not viewed as their Mass, but as a sacrificial rite performed by the priest for the benefit of the living and dead. Within this conceptual world of the early Middle Ages, the gifts for a Mass gradually took on a new meaning: they were given with an eye to obtaining the recompense of a Mass offered for the intention of the donor.

2. In the Eucharist of the first to the third century, the relation between liturgy and social justice was consciously expressed through the offering of material gifts. In the Middle Ages, the new understanding of the Mass prevented this relationship from coming to the foreground. For the Mass was really not seen as the place where the community manifests and realizes itself in an act of thanksgiving before God, even if this theme still found place in scientific theology; rather, the Mass itself had become an instrument in the hands of the clergy to meet the needs of the people.

3. The modern discussion of the meaning of gifts directly related to the offering of a Mass takes two directions in Catholic

theology. One interpretation relates to the traditional Eastern point of view already expressed in the third-century *Didascalia*. The other explanation draws on the conceptual world of the old Roman and North African Churches. In the first perspective, gifts are added to a unified sacrificial act performed by the priest on behalf of the people; in the second view, the gifts are a symbolic expression of the act of thanksgiving in which all co-offer the Eucharist.

Both viewpoints, however, favor the same basic understanding of the offering of material gifts directly related to the Mass: they signify the intention of the donor to integrate himself or herself more intimately into the prayer of thanksgiving. Therefore the offering of gifts expresses the consecration of one's whole life and work, including the fulfillment of social obligations "before God."

4. This new approach to the significance of the gifts offered "for a Mass" corresponds in great part to the understanding of the meaning of gifts presented in the liturgy of the early Church. Correspondingly, God's poor are singled out as the normal recipients. As this understanding of the meaning of the Eucharist and the gifts offered "for a Mass" or given in the liturgy penetrates the consciousness of priests and people, it will provide a new appreciation of the relation between worship and social justice. Furthermore, it will provide the theological basis for the laity to meet their social obligations in the liturgy and so bring a new commitment to social action in their daily lives.

VI. Practical Considerations

1. The catechesis of the Mass should emphasize that Christians are called on to consecrate themselves, their work, and the fruit thereof to God. It should further stress the relationship between the service of God in the liturgy and the service of humankind in the world.

2. The collections at the Eucharist should be interpreted as a

symbolic expression of this consecration to God. The use made of these collections should not be self-serving but should correspond to the wider horizon of the Christian community's social obligations. It should be taken for granted by the community that the normal recipients are God's poor. In this way the community is enabled consciously to actualize the relation between worship and social justice. Collections exclusively intended for church buildings, schools, etc., are more fittingly made in another context.

3. The old Roman offertory procession in many ways offers the best model for the presentation of gifts at the Eucharist. Also, the understanding of the meaning of the material gifts in this tradition seems to afford a better theological integration between liturgy and social justice. Symbolic of the co-offering of the people with the priest, they are integrated into the sacrificial prayer, not as an added sacrifice, but as the symbolic expression of the one sacrifice of praise and thanksgiving that includes both word and deed: "Through him [Jesus] let us continually offer God a sacrifice of praise, that is, the fruit of lips which acknowledge his name. Do not neglect good works and generosity: God is pleased with sacrifices of that kind" (Heb 13:15-16).

Symbols of Abundance, Symbols of Need

He who gives help to the lost is lost himself," declares Brecht in one of his plays.[1] Although Moltmann is no doubt correct in saying that Jesus' teaching is the reverse, what does our own experience seem to teach us? Might it not suggest ever so quietly that Brecht, and not Jesus, may be right after all? When one addresses Christians about familiar themes such as "service" and "need," caution is key. Few of us would characterize ourselves as totally insensitive to the gospel demand for "service" in response to the spiritual and temporal "needs" of the world. But the preceding sentence and the experience it may describe mean nothing until our working definitions of both "need" and "service" are retrieved. I say "retrieved" because our orthodox biblical definitions may only conceal quite unbiblical experience. It is that personal experience that might secretly rejoice that Brecht has at last said what we still dare not admit: "He who gives help to the lost is lost himself."

The function of an essay such as this, then, is more than

REGIS DUFFY, O.F.M., is associate professor at the Washington Theological Union. He holds a doctorate in sacramental theology from the Institut Catholique in Paris and has done post-doctoral work at the Sorbonne and the University of Würzburg. This paper was the keynote address at the sixth annual Notre Dame Conference on Pastoral Liturgy, June 1977.

informative. Information does not challenge the self-serving definitions of our experience nor the unredemptive praxis it may engender. Rather, our own experience of both service and need, symbolized in our praxis, must stand under the scrutiny of biblical symbols that capture the unsuspected need of a time-careless world that does not yet know the service it requires. My basic assumption, then, is this: Our redemptive need, and the service it cries out for, only begins to be "seen"[2] and accepted when we have learned to symbolize it. To facilitate such responsible symbolization, I will propose a series of theses in three interdependent areas: first, the biblical symbols of "hunger and thirst" and the correlative parabolic warnings about sinful satiety and false abundance; secondly, the prophetic action-word of "eating and drinking with the risen Lord" and its proclamation of disciple-need and world-need; finally, the potential of our worship and ministry to disclose, or indeed to hide, both our own and the world's need.

Symbols of False Abundance

Scriptural symbols suggest a rather uncompromising opening thesis: *The more subtle sin is to substitute false abundance for crying need, facile distribution for healing service.* Scripture suggests a negative image that will prepare us for the positive symbol of our need: *sinful satiety* which argues that it does not need God's fullness.[3]

Two parables capture and concretize this temptation: the rich fool (Luke 12:13-21) and the rich man and Lazarus (Luke 16:19-31). As in all parable, our security will be overturned, our satiety disproved.[4] Luke's rich fool, at first sight, seems rather responsible in preparing for his future. His sudden death as God's judgment is unsettling because it prompts the question: Is there no justified abundance? J.D.M. Derrett, in a particularly insightful analysis of the parable, brings us back to the root biblical image of God who is the "banker for the pious and stores up their good deeds for them to collect the capital in the World to come."[5] Therefore, he who gives to the poor lends to God. Another detail that Jesus could presume his Jewish audience to know is that whoever has a superabundance sees the name of the poor written upon it.[6] Jews were not to give out of their superfluity but out of their total income.[7] The man in the parable, however, is more interested in his long-range security than in the immediate need of the poor. Here, indeed, is false abundance, for the temptation to hoard obviates his need to be a guest of God's abundance. As verse 21 thunders, ". . . rich for themselves . . . not rich in God's sight." In brief, self-inflicted impoverishment blinds us to our need as well as to that of others.

A similar theme, pitched in a different key, is the parable of the rich man and Lazarus (Luke 16:19-31). Even the exceptional naming of the poor man — Lazarus ("God helps") — has a purpose.[8] As Jeremias correctly indicates, this parable is not a social commentary on the problem of poverty, nor does it support the notion that sickness is a punishment for sin. Indeed, it is the story of six brothers whose insensitivity both to their own and to others' needs will not permit them to accept even the searing truth of a revelation from God.[9] True need was never experienced. The Kingdom of God can offer little to one who believes that he has all.

Both parables could liberate Jesus' listeners to welcome the Kingdom. Only the needy will set up a lusty cry for God's gift; the satisfied can only chortle politely in appreciation for the unneeded thoughtfulness of God. Crossan is to the point: "Its [Luke 16:19ff.] metaphorical point was the reversal of expectation and situation, of value and judgment, which is the concomitant of the kingdom's advent."[10] In other words, these parables deliver the same message as the healing miracles of Jesus: the messianic sight to the blind and hearing to the deaf inevitably lead to our deeper and hitherto unsuspected needs. The credible sign that Jesus is still among us is that we refuse to say we are full when we are really starving, secure when we are truly in dire need. Only from such a starting point of more than academic need can we construct a theology of Church and sacrament.[11]

HUNGER AND THIRST: SYMBOLS OF ABUNDANCE

At this point, my second thesis should not startle anyone: *Only those who learn to hunger and thirst for God's feast now will enjoy it in the future.* If there is one symbol of need that spans both the Old and New Testaments, it is that of hunger and thirst. Christians are familiar with the beatitude (Matt 5:6; Luke 6:21).[12] But it is Matthew's "hungering and thirsting for right-eousness" that leads us back to the Old Testament images of need for God's mercy and presence.[13] Before Isaiah's panoramic image of God's feast of rich foods and vintage wines on the tops of the mountains (25:6), who would not begin to discover their hunger for his abundance?[14] This same scene is evoked in a transposed key of warning in Second Isaiah (65:13-14):

> See, my servants will eat, but you will hunger;
> See, my servants will drink, but you will thirst;
> See, my servants will be glad, but you will be abashed;
> See, my servants will shout with a joyous heart;
> But you will cry out with a sad heart,
>   and you will howl with a broken spirit.[15]

The parallel image of thirsting for wisdom (Prov 5:15; 9:5) is no less strong. Both images as actualized in God's covenant give us the cumulative symbol, *the food of the satisfied.* Isaiah 55 is the song of such covenant people.[16] And Isa 49:10 will assume new meaning when repeated in Rev 7:16:

> They shall not hunger anymore or thirst anymore,
> neither shall the sun
> or any scorching heat fall upon them,
> because the Lamb who is in the midst of the throne will shepherd them
> and guide them to springs of living water;
> and God will wipe away every tear from their eyes.[17]

The Johannine images of the need for water (John 4:14f.) lead
to the need for bread from heaven (John 6:26).[18] Commitment to
Jesus, in John's Gospel, is the only way to appease such hunger
and thirst. Yet our need cannot be dissociated from that of the
world. In a convergence with the Synoptics, this bread is a flesh
"for the life of the world" (John 6:51), an explanation of "for you"
(Luke 22:19) and "for the many" (Mark 14:24).[19]

Paradoxically, then, our need is only retrieved and redefined
to the degree that the needs of others are discovered. *Need is the
space for the growth of each one's gift today so that God's
tomorrow will not occur despite us.* Without the constant and
sometimes painful discovery of such need, how will we continue
to be committed?

In all these images and symbols, time lurks in the background.
Messianic feasts have not yet started, and for a good reason. The
fullness of God's future demands a present commitment to the
others. Revelation's promise (7:16) must use a future tense when
so many cling to their present false abundance. What Christian
who has prayed for his "daily bread" does not know this?
Jeremias reminds us, though, of Jerome's remark that Aramaic-
speaking Christians prayed, "Our bread for tomorrow give us
today."[20] Here too, then, we find that same realism. The symbols of God's abundance are useless if they have not already
begun to touch and transform the present time. As Jeremias con-
cludes, "Only when one has perceived that the petition asks for
bread in the fullest sense, for the bread of life, does the antithesis
between 'for tomorrow' and 'today' gain its full significance. . . . in a world of hunger and thirst, the disciples of
Jesus dare to utter this word 'today' — even now, even here,
already on this day, give us the bread of life."[21] In other words,
God makes the impossible possible. The hunger and thirst for
God's future feast will lead us back to today's commitment. Our
anticipation will be honest because time is not a selfish possession but the frame for needs yet to be served.[22] The feasts of
tomorrow are only for those who will hunger and thirst today.

The rich biblical symbols of hunger and thirst for the feast and of the food of the satisfied will be useless if they do not evoke from us our own experience and its symbols. The resulting new awareness of our redemptive needs will help us to redefine our service to others. These needs, in turn, can never be simply our private concerns. For our needs should redefine the discipleship of others even while those same needs call out our gifts for the other. When we re-examine our own stories, what are the symbols of our false abundance that might urge us to be better listeners of those parables against false satiety? What instances in our cyclic passages through life would point to a hunger and thirst for God's righteousness? When did the need of others re-key our own?

God's saving work has always preceded us so that we might gradually discover our shared and individual needs. This is what justification concretely means.[23] In learning to name our needs, we are dwarfed by the immensity of God's responding care. Psalm 107's staggering list of needs is answered by variations on the one theme of God's deliverance. Although the context of the psalm is obviously synagogue worship, there is a gentle dialectic that leads the congregation to look around at the others' needs in order to come back to their own. Paul Minear has not missed this nuance: "So, too, the psalm bespeaks a communal situation where many men join in a single song of joy; yet the experienced desolations and restorations are also individualized. By way of vivid language, worship serves to activate the eyes and ears of each worshiper, so that he becomes newly aware of the depths of need in himself and aware of how this need unites him to his fellows."[24]

God's justifying work, then, does not allow us to stare blindly at need or to listen deafly to cries wrung out of fragmented lives. On the contrary, it empowers the poor to be lavish, the deaf to listen, and the lame to heal. What other meaning would Mary's prophetic cry have: "He has put down the mighty from their thrones, and exalted those of low degree; he has filled the

hungry with good things and the rich he has sent empty away"
(Luke 1:52-53)?[25]

God's feast for the needy is no poetic image; it has the power
to gather those who were divided. Table-fellowship and community are not convoked for the private joy or salvation afforded but for the sake of all.[26] Need that does not lead to the
others divides us from them. Within this context, liberation
theology's insistence on the social context of need is important.[27]
If need is seen only from the vantage point of individual sin,
then we have not yet understood the positive and negative
teaching in the symbols of God's abundance or in the parabolic
warnings against false satiety. We are not yet ready, then, for
the feast of God's unity, because the need that separates us has
not become the need that binds us.

Prophetic Service and Disciple-Need

Service could not be described until biblical symbols enlarged
our definition of need. Now an opening thesis about such service
may be proposed: *Our service must be as prophetic as our need
is redemptive. For service not only alleviates but reveals and
clarifies the depth of our individual and shared need.*

Prophecy always introduces us into impossible situations and
then proceeds to show us how God alone makes them possible.
True need would never be uncovered without prophecy. More
important, true need could not be endured if prophetic hope did
not rob us of our excuses. For prophecy does not exist apart
from the wounded people who hear it.[28] They themselves are the
evidence of how God's presence-filled word renews even where
nothing was expected. And it is the continuing legacy of New
Testament prophets both to take issue with our too narrow
definitions of need and service and to give us new reason to cry
to God with hope.[29]

Nor can prophecy be separated from the nature of discipleship. A disciple cannot proclaim the Kingdom if he has not

aroused a hunger and thirst for God's righteousness. Such new need, such evangelical dissatisfaction, is not the result of relevant preaching but of power-filled prophecy of the disciple. This is the true service of the prophet that questions our own.[30] The only assurance that such disciple-service is redemptive is when new responsibility for both needs and service occurs.

In an initial thesis, sin was pinpointed as the source of our false abundance and our non-service. The corollary is, of course, irresponsibility. It allows for that curious group of people who love to read eschatology but who refuse to take part in it. They are the "Kingdom watchers" who hide their gifts and their need, like the servant with one talent (Matt 25:14-30), under the irresponsible contours of their lives. Tomorrow's bread becomes stale in their hands even today. Yet the power of God's word is such that these very people can be freed up to be responsible disciples.

Nowhere is this better seen than in the mutual master-disciple relationship, as noted by Daube. He points out that not only is Jesus held responsible for the actions of his disciples but they are likewise held responsible for his.[31] I would venture a further reflection. The instances of such mutual responsibility (why the disciples do not fast[32] and do pluck corn on the Sabbath,[33] why they eat with unwashed hands[34] or why the Master has table-fellowship with sinners[35]) underscore the priorities of the Kingdom and thus the revealed needs of those who would welcome it.

Although legalism or scandal may have prompted the questions, the underlying motivation in the conduct of Jesus and his friends, I submit, is grounded in a new awareness of what counts. Legalism permits false need to replace the true need. Legalism has no need for God's abundance, since it feels assured of God's "justice." But this suggestion of disciple-need finds its best support in the question of table-fellowship with sinners. The implicit need and service of these situations helped simple fishermen to eventually become disciples and prophets.

The significance and the scandal of Jesus' feasting with sinners have both appropriately received much exegetical comment.[36] A strong case might be made for understanding Jesus' action-word of eating with sinners as a prophetic sign (*ot*).[37] This would mean that such meals were an anticipation of God's eschatological feast, but they were more than that.[38] They would not only remind sinners of the symbols of God's abundance but *enable them to hunger and thirst for the reality of the symbols.* The *berakoth* (praise-thanks) at such meals are evocative of need and call for more than blessing of bread and wine as such. Promises of messianic or eschatological feasts are dangerous if they are not first accepted within the humble feasting of sinners in the presence of God; dangerous, too, if commitment and need are not coupled as response at such feasts.

But what of those disciples of Jesus who perhaps went along rather reluctantly to such feasts? Is it true, as Moltmann has recently contended, that for the feasting sinners the meal means acceptance and justification, while for the feasting disciples it is participation in Jesus' mission of seeking the poor?[39] That position would seem to give us "saved" disciples and justified but un-discipled sinners at the end of meals. In that case, the last state of both groups would then be worse than the first. Rather, I suspect that the disciples learned their own need only as they learned to serve like the Master at such meals. Yes, discipleship was indeed formed at these tables, but only to the extent that a Simon Peter and Simon the Pharisee (Luke 7:36ff.) were aware of their shared need as much as the scorned woman washing Jesus' feet at the same meal. Even the sons of Zebedee, after so many such meals, had not yet learned how to ask for the endless feast but only for unending non-service.[40]

To return, then, to the mutual responsibility of master-disciple: If disciples must answer for why the masters eat with sinners, they can only do so because their need has begotten service, and their service, need. Our previous thesis will be the best summary: *Our service must be as prophetic as our need is redemptive. For service not only alleviates but reveals and clarifies the depth of our individual and shared need.*

THE POST-EASTER PROPHETS

The pre-Easter meals of Jesus with sinners can have no full meaning apart from the post-Easter meals with disciples. This might be developed in another thesis: *The post-Easter prophets of each age must learn to sit down as sinner-disciples to eat and drink with a risen Lord if they are to rise up as servant-prophets for their world.*

While the faith-experience and practice of the early Christian community contributed to the shaping of these mainly Lucan and Johannine accounts,[41] the meals with the risen Lord represent more than Eucharistic praxis projected back into these chapters. The eschatological dimension is certainly there.[42] Moreover, a complementary messianic meal dimension seems to be the point of the fish menu in the post-Easter meals of Luke and John.[43] Nor is it a coincidence that early Christian iconography uses post-Easter bread and fish (and not bread and wine) as the standard symbol for the Eucharist.[44] In brief, the larger context of these meal scenes is redemptive, and the meal symbol is the carrier for a new definition of God's abundance in the face of failed discipleship. The early Church, after all, did not phrase its redemptive questions in the theoretical fashion of a Pannenberg or Rahner but concretely, in wondering what effect a truly risen Lord could now have on the likes of a Peter, James, or John.

Further, Lebeau is perhaps correct in suggesting that wine, a privileged eschatological symbol, is missing in these post-Easter meals because "the Spirit had not yet been given" (John 7:39).[45] The exception seems to support this insight. Peter's post-Pentecost argument that the apostles are witnesses to a risen Lord appeals to the fact that they both ate *and drank* with him after the Resurrection (Acts 10:41). The point: not only is the

Spirit now given but given to *those who are sent*.[46] The post-Easter meals, then, must illustrate the healing pedagogy of a Lord whose victory over death will be tested and vindicated in the disciple-commitment and service of faltering people.

The pre-Easter meals, too, had demanded such commitment. As one exegete reminds us: "To eat with him was to become vulnerable to divine judgment and to divine grace. Action and speech at table became an index to ultimate destiny, for every component of the good news was illustrated at one of these occasions."[47] But these meals of promise and abundance had not precluded later denials, incomprehension, and self-serving disappointment.

From this viewpoint, that post-Easter breakfast conversation between Jesus and Peter assumes new meaning (John 21:15-23). After Jesus has questioned Peter's love for him and then charged him with service ("feed/shepherd my lambs/sheep"—John 21:15-17), he prophesies that although Peter, as a *neōteros* ("young person"), did what he chose, as an old person (*gerases*) he will be led where he does not want to go. The usual exegesis of this passage is a prediction of Peter's eventual martyrdom, but Elliott has made a strong case for an additional meaning. *Neōteros* would refer to the early stage of Peter's discipleship, and "old age" to ". . . the full submission to the work and plan of God . . . which marks Peter's Christian and apostolic maturity in contrast to the self-determination characteristic of Peter's Christian 'adolescence.'"[48]

Meals of abundance, then, do not lead to the redemptive service of discipleship if the gradual conversions from "young" to "old" are not made. The post-Easter questions of disciple-love and "feeding the sheep" implicitly ask harder questions about new awareness of needs, and thus of service.[49] Disciple-proclamation of old needs answered by the new event of the Resurrection is prophetic. But the prophet is one who not only makes actual the event in his own environment but *lives* the event.[50] He can only bridge the distance between a risen and ascended Lord and his own contemporaries if his life is marked by the many passages that conversion is. The training of prophetic people is a function, therefore, of these resurrection accounts with their meals of abundance and their demands for committed belief and service.[51]

To sit with Jesus at the table of a Zacchaeus (Luke 19:5) in the early days of discipleship might have been perplexing for a Peter or a James. To eat and drink with an abstaining Master at that final meal might have been deeply troubling. But far more difficult were the reconciliation meals with a Lord who rose so that they might rise, but only after dying. "Can you drink the cup that I am about to drink?" (Matt 20:22) no longer admits of the glib pre-Easter answer of naive disciples: "We can."[52] For to accept the continuing cup is to ask for the reconciliation that only sinners and the poor know the need of. The disciple is formed in the midst of such need. Like the nameless co-guest at the Pharisee's feast who hears Jesus' parable about places at the wedding feast and then responds in a *berakah* ("How happy are those who will sit at the table in the Kingdom of God"—Luke 14:15), the disciple learns to hunger and thirst because deep need has been accepted and committed service pledged. Moltmann is right:

> Anyone who celebrates the Lord's supper in a world of hunger and oppression does so in complete solidarity with the hopes and suffering of all men, because he believes that the Messiah invites all men to his table and because he hopes they will all sit at the table with him. In the mysteries, the feast separates the initiated from the rest of the world. But Christ's messianic feast makes its participants one with the physically and spiritually hungry all over the world.[53]

To summarize this second section on the needs and service of post-Easter prophets, we can do no better than to return to that forceful little parable about two groups of children, one of which wants to play "wedding," and the other, "funeral" (Matt 11:16-19). The parable is perhaps addressed to the lazy spectators of salvation who perversely want a John the Baptizer to dance and a Jesus to lament so that they may have an excuse to remain dissatisfied and uncommitted.[54] Interestingly, Jesus phrases the complaint of these contemporaries against him: "Look at this man! He is a glutton and a drunkard, a friend of tax collectors and sinners" (v. 19).

The parable might serve as a point of reference in our own search for our symbols of abundance (true or false), for our hunger and thirst. As we look down the tables of our own lives, have our failed expectations gradually become the explanation of our failed ministries? Have our own needs yet to be retrieved because the scandal of the table companions the Lord has given us was too great? Does the faltering discipleship of other Peters or Thomases become the reasoned excuse for the dearth of our post-Easter meals and their resulting prophetic service? Would our contemporaries even think of saying of us: "Why, look at this man, that woman! A glutton and a drunkard, a friend of tax collectors and sinners"? Where have all the symbols of abundance gone — in our lives?

Feasts Without Cause?

Feasts without cause can be misleading, if not dangerous. After all, the only reason for beginning such feasts of God's abundance even now would be if our shared need, more deeply acknowledged, impelled us to more prophetic service. Recently Gerhard Martin, in calling for "fest" (literally "feast," as opposed to a "party") as a transformation of everyday, reminded us that there are unreal models of feasting.[55] These are the pseudo-celebrations that either separate feast from everyday life or try to equate daily life with feast. He argues for a messianic understanding of feast where ". . . the ordinary situation becomes the kingdom of God."[56]

The problem, of course, is that the "ordinary situations" of our life are quite complex. We cannot appreciate, appropriate, or symbolize that complexity out of theological theories of need, service, and kingdom. The symbol of a Mother Teresa of Calcutta bent over the teeming sick and poor leaves such theories in disarray. Charles Davis has aptly summed up the underlying problem: ". . . in the church there is at present theory without practice and practice without theory."[57] Praxis, as used in contemporary theology, represents the "doing" in our lives and is connected with the shared stories we live and the shared need those stories tell.[58] Davis is referring to an isolation between our everyday situation and what we should be learning, between our story fragments and our symbols of feast. When this occurs, the Kingdom of God and its feasts are reduced to a literally incredible theory, because our praxis does not even betray the needs that would make such a Kingdom necessary. Anouilh is right when in his screenplay he has Vincent De Paul say to a young sister about to go out and serve in the slums of Paris: "The poor will not forgive you your gift of bread if you do not give it with love." For true Christian love, we have contended, comes out of a praxis of mutual need and service that requires constant revision of our theories of both fast and feast.

To focus the question more sharply: What type of life-praxis would prepare us for the feast coming to meet us?[59] Life-praxis refers to the fact that my personal identity is lived out in a process in which my unique self interacts with a social group. Jesus' life-praxis should have an inner connection with the symbol he lived: table-fellowship and its promise of God's feast. Fiorenza, in his search for a viable christology that would better take into account the violent death of Jesus, suggests a twofold solidarity evident in the life-praxis of Jesus. "This double solidarity is revealed in his proclamation of the will of the Father and his preaching of the Kingdom of God as well as in his forgiving of sins, performance of exorcisms, and miraculous healings."[60] Fiorenza then goes on to maintain that it was Jesus' life-praxis as a whole (relations with both the Father and the outcasts) that called for his death. His self-identity as witnessed in his life-praxis radically challenged the false abundance that is all a world of sin can offer. Yes, he had to be killed for being who he was and doing what he did.[61]

I should like to go a step further and apply this to our own situation in the form of another thesis: *Only a life-praxis that continually redefines need and service within its complex social context can prophetically challenge the false feasts of its age. If our life-praxis does not contain such a challenge, then we will be as bored with God's final feast as we have been satisfied with our current meager hunger and thirst for his righteousness.*

An indication of how successful those post-Easter meals of reconciliation really were is the tradition of the Christian Church that most of those disciples were killed because their own life-praxis, like that of the Master, was disturbing the hunger and thirst of their time. These were not people capable of using critical social theory to analyze the complex needs of their time and the ministry it would require; rather, those final meals summarized and symbolized for them also the solidarity with the Father and with others. That solidarity shaped itself into a gradual life-praxis that could not be tolerated by the world. In living such a life, they were constantly learning how to sit at the table with others. Even the sons of Zebedee had less time, perhaps, to worry about their places at the final banquet when there was so much hunger and thirst at the tables of their contemporaries.

Each age has contributed some theories and much praxis on need and service, presumably based on the gospel. Paul's collection for the needy Church in Jerusalem still goes on. Martin of Tours is still splitting that military cloak. Francis is kissing the leper again and again. And how many sick does Mother Teresa still have to care for? All these individuals died many small deaths because of their life-praxis, which touched and troubled their contemporaries. Theirs was no meager hunger and thirst. These witnesses, like the poor themselves, are always with us so that we may better remember the solidarity of need and service, so that we might wonder why our life-praxis troubles no one these days.

A more difficult, even bewildering, dimension of the problem, however, is the Christian community as a group. What were the needs and service that the Christian communities of Nazi Germany should have responded to? What shape should the life-praxis of a Christian community, situated in a country where human rights are scorned, have? Papal or episcopal theories of need and service do not rescue the credibility of the gospel if the shared ecclesial life-praxis of Christians is no match for their more zealous humanist or Marxist contemporaries. I have no solution for this, only a reminder. Sociologists of our age will not excuse themselves so easily from the burden of understanding how the complications of action and experience, rooted in the unity of life context, demand not only better theory but more committed life-praxis.[62] Nor should we.

Feasts without cause, therefore, only come out of the individual and communal life-praxis that excuses itself from the complexity of the crowd that continues to press in on us from all sides as it did the Master. What to do if one has only five fish to feed so many can be as complicated for one group of disciples as what to do in South Africa can be for later groups. Yet, the Master's response is the same in both cases: "You yourselves give them something to eat" (Matt 14:16).

RESPONSIBLE FEASTS

Ideally, liturgical *pietas* is not a posture but a complex and responsive attitude not only toward God but also toward his world.[63] The worship that such piety elicits brings us back to our own and others' need with new awareness. But, as already suggested, where there is such need, responsible service cannot be far behind. As a thesis, it might read: *We can only worship God because our need is constantly answered by his free and freeing gift (justification), and others' need tests the gift we have been freely given.*

The dangers of a worship that is less than this should be obvious. Long ago Bonhoeffer eloquently spelled out the profound impact that true worshipers have on their world.[64] Liberation theology has warned us of those who believe in a sacramental "efficacy" that excuses them from gospel responsibility.[65] Political theology reviews the history of the gradual sacralization of a worship that sometimes seemed to support godless power structures more willingly than a kingdom in search of a feast.[66] From various concerns, all these voices recall the same truth: We worship not only to have strength to feed the needy but also to be able, in the first place, even to recognize them.[67]

If worship is to clarify our individual and shared life-praxis in its proper social situation so that we might better see our needy creation, still groaning, it will not be done apart from our own intertwined stories. Such stories, more responsibly told, strengthen us for more responsibility. Such stories, resulting in more honest cries to God, will give us a hunger and thirst for redemptive unity, the only assurance we have that the feast is not far off. Such worship will evoke the commitment that sends us out into the highways and byways, looking for the blind and the lame of our world so that the banquet hall will be full (Luke 14:21-23) and the feast may begin.[68]

God's free and freeing gift of love, responsive to our deepest need, is called justification. When we worship, our sacred ground and space is his justification. Worship transforms that abstract term into the symbols of our need, which God answers with the demand for responsible service. Here, then, is both the test of experienced justification and the sourcebook for the world's need: a worship that will not leave us with our small serenities, a worship that will send us back to the post-Easter meals yet to be eaten. This is a worship that returns us to a world that is not yet enough God's, not only to eat with the outcasts but even to be worthy to be "reckoned with transgressors."[69] This is the worship that begets a priesthood of the faithful that is not the privilege of the dogmatically correct but,

as recent exegesis reminds us, the result of serving and the suffering it ensures.[70]

FROM THE EAST AND THE WEST

But must all the guests invited to the feast bring a gift? In other
words, if all are called to the Kingdom's feast-without-end, is it
only the Christian that brings the gift of service? Matthew's
answer (8:5-13) is still an unsettling one. He recounts the Roman
officer's request for the healing of his servant. So great is his confidence in Jesus' word that the officer will not permit him to dis-
place himself. Jesus' response to such faith captures both the joy
and the judgment of the feast: "Many will come from the east
and the west and will sit at the table in the kingdom of heaven
. . . . But the sons of the Kingdom will be thrown out into the
darkness outside. . . ." (vv. 11–12). The Gentiles, the world, at
the eschatological banquet? Yes, if they had a faith rooted in
need. Schweizer's remark is apt: ". . . the officer is open to expect everything from him, even what is apparently impossible.
Thus what he says expresses both his awareness and his own
emptiness and the daring leap that counts concretely on the
power of God."[71] In stark contrast, the "sons of the Kingdom"
and their false abundance is a sharp reference to the Christian
community of Matthew's time.[72]

Our need, it has been argued, cannot be known apart from
our fellow disciple-prophets. Nor can that beloved community
itself deserve more than Matthew's warning if it will not be open
to the prophets that people all of God's world.[73] God's work
always precedes us in our service. We should not be surprised,
then, by the prophetic faith of the non-Christian or "unbeliever"
who seems to know better definitions of need and service than
we ourselves do. We should rejoice that our need has been
healed by their service.[74]

We have come full circle. "He who gives help to the lost is lost
himself," said Brecht. And what do we say? The parables against

false abundance, the symbols of hunger and thirst for the feast coming to meet us, are wasted upon us if they do not question our lived experience. After all, has not the work of God preceded us even there?

For our own symbol-building and parable-making, I offer these summary questions. What are our own signs of false abundance, of facile distribution? What are the hungers and thirsts that transform the "now" of our current lives? What is the redemptive unity we currently work for that would make the guest list of God's future feast? What service, responsive to the need of the world, has opened our eyes, loosed our tongues, freed our limbs to walk? When last, in the continuing education of our current lives, did we sit at post-Easter meals, eat the fish of promise, the bread of tomorrow today? When last, in worship, did God's free gift and our new need converge so that we "saw" the other? When last did the world's need surprise us enough to send us back to our own need with a startled cry of recognition?

When last did we have the courage to bless (*berakah*) God with that ancient Passover cry: *"So may Yahweh our God and the God of our fathers bring us in peace to other set feasts which are coming to meet us"*?[75]

NOTES

Searle: SERVING THE LORD WITH JUSTICE, pp. 13–35.

1. "The Fisher King," a retelling by Ann Himmler based on Wolfram von Eschenbach's *Parzival,* in *Parabola* 3, no. 2 (1978) 16–22.

2. On the need to return to the classical treatment of justice in terms of order, see D. Burrell, "Justice . . . What Is It All About?" *Occasional Papers on Catholic Higher Education* 4, no. 2 (Winter 1978) 12–17.

3. For an illuminating discussion of More and the law, see S. Hauerwas and T. L. Shaffer, "Hope Faces Power: Thomas More and the King of England," *Soundings* 61, no. 4 (Winter 1978) 456–79.

4. *Epistle to Diognetus,* trans. H. G. Meechan (Manchester University Press, 1949) 78–80.

5. *La tradition apostolique* 20, ed. Bernard Botte (Paris: Editions du Cerf, 1968²) 78.

6. *Prex Eucharistica,* ed. A. Hänggi and I. Pahl (Fribourg: Editions Universitaires, 1968) 363.

7. *Summa Theologiae* II-II, q. 81 art. 1. See also art. 4.

8. Psalm 95, the invitatory psalm of the Liturgy of the Hours.

9. For a psychological study of this question from a Jungian perspective, see A. Guggenbuhl-Craig, *Power in the Helping Professions* (New York: Spring Publications, 1971).

10. John Moiser, "A Promise of Plenty: The Eucharist as Social Critique," *Downside Review* 91, no. 305 (October 1973) 298–305.

11. For a summary of views on this matter, see David Hollenbach's excellent article "A Prophetic Church and the Catholic Sacramental Imagination," *The Faith That Does Justice,* ed. John C. Haughey (New York: Paulist Press, 1977) 234–63.

12. On the subversive character of parable, see John D. Crossan, *The Dark Interval* (Niles, Ill.: Argus Communications, 1975).

13. Alexander Schmemann, "Sacrifice and Worship," *Parabola* 3, no. 2 (Winter 1978) 65.

14. Fedor Dostoyevsky, *The Brothers Karamazov,* trans. D. Magarshack (Harmondsworth: Penguin Books) 2:761–62.

Burghardt: PREACHING THE JUST WORD, pp. 36–52.

1. See the *Washington Star,* May 26, 1979, D-1 and D-2; quotation at D-2.

2. *Ibid.*

3. *Ibid.*

4. T. Howland Sanks, S.J., and Brian H. Smith, S.J., "Liberation Ecclesiology: Praxis, Theory, Praxis," *Theological Studies* 38 (1977) 24.

5. George G. Higgins, "The Church and Social Concerns," syndicated col-
umn, excerpted from *One Voice* (Diocese of Birmingham, Ala.), April 27, 1979,
4.

6. As cited by Higgins, *ibid.*

7. Pius XII, *Allocutio ad cultores historiae et artis*, May 9, 1956 (*AAS* 48
[1956] 212).

8. *Apostolicam actuositatem*, no. 5; see also no. 7. In response to this quotation, one might dredge up the affirmation of *Gaudium et spes*, no. 42: "Christ, to
be sure, gave his Church no proper mission in the political, economic, or social
order. The purpose which he set before it is a religious one. . . ." Here the
crucial terms are *missio propria* and *finis . . . ordinis religiosi.* Discussion of
these phrases is not possible here, but two observations seem to be in order. (1)
GS 42 is not excluding the Christian community from playing a significant,
transforming role in the social, economic, and political orders. Such an interpretation would make nonsense out of Part 1, chapter 4. The text reaffirms the
legitimate autonomy that belongs to the temporal order. For the historical
background of this chapter (nos. 40–45) and an insightful presentation of its
meaning, see Yves Congar's chapter "The Role of the Church in the Modern
World," in Herbert Vorgrimler, ed., *Commentary on the Documents of Vatican
II* 5 (New York: Herder and Herder, 1969) 202–23. For example, "The Church's
function comprises everything human. . . . Consequently the Church must not
be restricted to a 'religious' domain, identical in practice with public worship"
(213). (2) There is a problem on what "Church" means in chapter 4. Charles
Moeller argues, from the proposed amendments, that whereas in chapters 1 to 3
it means "the People of God," in chapter 4 it refers to the hierarchy (*ibid.*, 61–62).
Congar (*ibid.*, 211 and 214 [see n. 28 for pertinent *relatio*]), without alluding to
Moeller's position, says the Church in chapter 4 is "the People of God," "the
social body." The difference in interpretation of "Church" is obviously not irrele-
vant to one's understanding of the Church's mission.

9. 1971 Synod of Bishops, *De iustitia in mundo* (Vatican Press, 1971), Introduction, p. 5. One may argue whether "constitutive" in the document means "integral" or "essential" (the 1976 document of the International Theological Commission, "Human Development & Christian Salvation," trans. Walter J. Burghardt, S.J., *Origins* 7, no. 20 [Nov. 3, 1977] 311, states that "it seems more accurate to interpret [*ratio constitutiva*] as meaning an integral part, not an essential part" [IV] — a discussable affirmation). What is beyond argument is that the
Synod saw the search for justice as inseparable from the preaching of the gospel.

10. 1974 Synod of Bishops, "Human Rights and Reconciliation," *Origins* 4
(1974) 318.

11. "Human Development & Christian Salvation" IV (translation in *Origins* 7
[1977] 310–11).

12. For a careful appraisal of "what the Old and New Testaments have to say
about the relationship between salvation and human welfare, between salvation
and human rights," see the document of the ITC (n. 9 above), III (translation in

Origins 309-10). See also *The Social Message of the Gospels*, ed. Franz Böckle, Concilium 35 (New York: Paulist Press, 1968).

13. Address of Pope John Paul II opening the deliberations of the Third Assembly of Latin American Bishops, Puebla, January 28, 1979, III, 2. An English translation is available in *Origins 8*, no. 34 (Feb. 8, 1979) 530-38; but I have not used it for the passage quoted, because it translates *indispensable* as "essential" (536), apparently unaware of the problem to which I allude in n. 9 above. I take it that the Pope and/or his speechwriter consciously avoided a philosophical interpretation of the 1971 Synod's *ratio constitutiva;* it is enough that a facet of the Church's evangelizing mission be described as something that the Church may not refuse to do; it is not capable of being dispensed with; the Church cannot be released from this obligation. The Pope goes on to cite Paul VI's *Evangelii nuntiandi,* no. 29: "evangelization would not be complete if it did not take into account the unceasing interplay of the Gospel and of man's concrete life, both personal and social" (*Origins* 536).

14. On this see my "A Theologian's Challenge to Liturgy," *Theological Studies* 35 (1974) 233-48, at 240-44.

15. Brian Wicker, "Ritual and Culture: Some Dimensions of the Problem Today," in James D. Shaughnessy, ed., *The Roots of Ritual* (Grand Rapids: Eerdmans, 1973) 17. See also George G. Higgins, "The Mass and Political Order," *Proceedings of the Liturgical Conference,* Worcester, Mass., August 1955: "Shortly after World War II an extremely well-informed German priest told me, on what I am prepared to accept as reliable evidence, that the Nazis, far from being worried about the pre-war growth of the liturgical movement in Germany, secretly encouraged it. According to my informant, they felt that an intense preoccupation with the liturgy would serve to distract the attention of Catholics and make them less inclined to engage in political action. Whether this report is accurate or not, the record will show, I think, that some of those most actively engaged in the liturgical movement not only in Germany but in other countries as well did make the mistake of ignoring political and social problems or, even worse, of at least passively favoring political programs which they should have actively opposed" (130-31).

16. Tissa Balasuriya, O.M.I., *The Eucharist and Human Liberation* (Maryknoll, N.Y.: Orbis Books, 1979).

17. Joseph Gelineau, "Celebrating the Paschal Liberation," in *Politics and Liturgy,* ed. Herman Schmidt and David Power, Concilium 92 (New York: Herder and Herder, 1974) 107.

18. "Editorial," *ibid.,* 8.

19. Gelineau, "Celebrating the Paschal Liberation," 107.

20. *Ibid.,* 111.

21. Higgins, "The Mass and Political Order," 133.

22. Yves Congar, O.P., "Sacramental Worship and Preaching," in *The Renewal of Preaching: Theory and Practice,* Concilium 33 (New York: Paulist Press, 1968) 60.

23. *Ibid.*, 54.

24. See *ibid.*, 55–56; also my "The Word Made Flesh Today," *New Catholic World* 221 (1978) 116–25, at 122.

25. Ambrose, *Letter 20*, 19.

26. See Socrates, *Church History* 6, 18; Sozomen, *Church History* 8, 20.

27. John Paul II, Homily, Mass in Independence Plaza, Santo Domingo, Jan. 25, 1979 (*Origins* 8, 34 [Feb. 8, 1979] 543). I am aware that the Pope does go on to speak of a "more divine world" as well, "the vertical orientation of evangelization" (*ibid.*).

28. Karl Rahner, S.J., *The Shape of the Church to Come* (London: SPCK, 1974) 77.

29. *Ibid.*, 76.

30. See my *Seven Hungers of the Human Family* (Washington, D.C.: United States Catholic Conference, 1976) 8–15, especially 11–13.

31. See *Time* 113, no. 23 (June 4, 1979) 24.

32. See *ibid.*, 69.

33. George Higgins, "The Problems in Preaching: Politics/What Place in Church?" *Origins* 2, no. 13 (Sept. 21, 1972) 213. The whole article (207, 212–16) merits reading for its wedding of the theoretical and the practical, based on the respected author's long and varied experience.

34. Quoted by Higgins, *ibid.*, 216.

35. See "The Word Made Flesh Today" (n. 24 above) 125.

36. Quoted by Joel Porte, "'I Am Not the Man You Take Me For,'" *Harvard Magazine* 81, no. 5 (May–June 1979) 50.

37. *Ibid.*, 50–51.

Kilmartin: THE SACRIFICE OF THANKSGIVING AND SOCIAL JUSTICE, pp. 53–71.

1. A. Flannery, ed., *Vatican Council II: The Conciliar and Post Conciliar Documents* (Collegeville, Minn.: Liturgical Press, 1975) 929–30.

2. *Ibid.*, 930.

3. *Ibid.*, 932.

4. *Ibid.*, 940–45.

5. *Ibid.*, 350.

6. *Ibid.*, 362.

7. *Ibid.*, 107.

8. The *Didache*, a Church order of the early second century, calls the Christian meal *eucharistia* (9, 1) and states that Christians gather on Sunday to "break bread and give thanks" (*eucharistein*—14, 1). The contemporary bishop of Antioch, Ignatius, applies *eucharistia* to the holy bread (*Letter to the Smyrnaeans 7*, 1). Four decades later Justin Martyr refers to the cultic meal as *eucharistia* (*First Apology* 65, 3–5; 67, 7) and also says: "We call this food *eucharistia.* . . . made *eucharistia* by the prayer of the word. . . ." (*First Apology* 66, 1ff.).

In the second-century orthodox Churches, the prayer of praise and thanksgiving is considered both an earthly-human act and a pneumatic action of the Word of God — both a thanksgiving and a blessing. The same holds true for the bread and wine. They are considered symbols of the community's thanksgiving for God's gifts of creation and redemption as well as of the blessings that come from God, especially in the liturgical celebration under the form of the sacrament of the Word-made-flesh (see Justin Martyr, *First Apology* 66).

The great theologian of the third century, Origen, actually systematizes this traditional understanding of the ecclesial-liturgical word and the sacrament of the Body and Blood of Jesus Christ. His particular theological outlook, however, leads him to devaluate to some degree the sacrament of the Body and Blood vis-à-vis the "verbal presence" of the Logos (see L. Lees, *Wort und Eucharistie bei Origenes: Zur Spiritualisierung des Eucharistieverständnis*, Innsbrucker theologische Studien I [Innsbruck: Tyrolia, 1978] 37-214).

9. Tertullian mentions the custom of the annual presentation of an oblation for the dead on the anniversary of their death (*De corona* 4, 1). His question directed to a man who marries after the death of his first wife makes clear that through this offering the deceased is joined to the community as offerer of the Eucharist: "Will you stand then before the Lord with both wives whom you commend in the prayer? And will you offer for the two and recommend each of the two through the priest?" (*De exhortatione castitatis* 11, 1ff.).

In the same tradition, Cyprian, bishop of Carthage, quotes the regulation of a recently held council (before the middle of the third century) that forbids a Christian to engage a priest as executor of his will. The punishment for disobedience is stipulated: ". . . no gift should be offered for him, nor sacrifice celebrated for his falling asleep. For he has not merited to be named at the altar of God in the prayer of the priest. . . ." Because of this rule, Cyprian orders, in the case of Victor, who violated the canon, that "no oblation be made for his falling asleep . . . or any prayer in his name find place in the church" (*Letter* 1, 2). In the canonical rule, *oblatio* and *sacrificium* are distinguished but treated alike. So closely are they connected that Cyprian subsumes them both under *oblatio*. Moreover, it should be noted that *oblatio* and the reading of the name are not considered to be a form of intercession and help for the soul. Both actions have place also in the case of a martyr.

10. Justin Martyr refers to a collection made for the needy at the Eucharist, although he does not call it a sacrifice (*First Apology* 67, 1). The contemporary bishop of Smyrna, Polycarp, speaks of widows as "an altar of God" (*Letter to the Philippians* II, 4, 3). Being of ecclesiastical rank, widows live from the offerings of believers and are likened to an altar on which gifts are presented to God. Here no immediate connection with the Eucharist is envisioned. However, Cyprian refers to gifts presented at the Eucharist as *"sacrificium"* (*De opere et eleemosynis* 15) or as *"sacrificium Christi"* (*Letters* 1, 2; 12, 9; 63, 9).

11. F. X. Funk, *Didascalia et Constitutiones Apostolorum* II (Paderborn, 1905) 26, 2ff.; E. Tidner, *Didascalia Apostolorum. Canonum ecclesiasticorum. Traditionis Apostolicae versiones latinae*, Texte und Untersuchungen 75 (Berlin, 1963) 41.

12. Funk, loc. cit.

13. See n. 3 above.

14. A. Mayer, Triebkräfte und Grundlinien der Entstehung des Messstipendiums, Münchener theologische Studien III: Kanonistische Abteilung 34 (St. Ottilien: Eos, 1976) 75–81; 104–8.

15. Ibid., 135–40.

16. Isidore of Seville (d. 633) can serve as witness for the general practice of the time. He states that "the offering for the repose of deceased believers or praying for them is the tradition of the apostles in our estimation, because it is practiced throughout the whole world" (De ecclesiasticis officiis I, 18, 11; PL 83:757).

17. In the ninth century, the understanding of the priest as representative of the people who co-offer with him was still somewhat alive. A text formerly ascribed to Alcuin states that the priest at the Sursum corda commands the faithful to lift up their hearts "in order that I may be able to offer worthily the sacrifice which you have given to me to present to God (De divinis officiis 40; PL 101:1252D). According to Amalar of Metz, it is the "gift of the whole people" that is offered "through the hands of the priest" (Liber officialis III, 19, 4, 17, 36, in J. M. Hanssens, Amalarii episcopi opera liturgica omnia, Studi e Testi 139 [Vatican City, 1948] 2:312, 316, 332).

18. Mayer, op. cit., 190–91.

19. Ibid., 194.

20. Ibid., 213–17.

21. For example, in the development of the theology of the sacrament of penance, indulgences, and the "treasury of the Church."

22. Already in the ninth century, a synod at Rome (826), under Pope Eugene II, stated that priests should accept the gifts of all who come to Mass. As mediators of God and men, priests must be there for all; otherwise it would appear as if the Redeemer does not accept the petition of all (can. 17; Mansi 14:1005). This legislation presupposed that it is determined beforehand who can be considered offerers at Mass. It shows that the priest alone was considered the active subject of the offering and drew others into his activity.

23. Paschasius Radbertus (d. 859), abbot of Corbie, wrote the first extended treatise on the Eucharist between 831 and 833. Influenced by a strong patristic tradition exemplified by the Antiochene school, he affirmed both the mystery presence of the sacrifice of the Cross in the Mass and the identity of the Eucharistic body with the glorified historical body of Jesus Christ. This theology was considered new by some respected theologians such as Rabanus Maurus (Poenitentiale 33; PL 110:493). Ratramnus (d. 869), another monk of Corbie, replied to a request for clarification of Eucharistic theology made by Emperor Charles the Bald. He opposed Paschasius' treatise. Showing greater affinity for the traditional Augustinian position, he interpreted the elements as signs that are not identical with the glorified historical body of the Redeemer. Also, for him the liturgy of the Mass refers to but does not contain the actual presence of the mystery of the redemptive Passion itself. See F. Pratzner, Messe und Kreutzesopfer: Die Krise der sakramentalen Idee bei Luther und der mittelalterlichen

Scholastik, Wiener Beiträge zur Theologie 29 (Vienna: Herder, 1970) 119–32), who traces the roots of the crisis over the concept of sacrament back to the Carolingian period.

24. Pratzner, *op. cit.*, 119–32.

25. *Ibid.*, 94–98; also Th. Schneider, "Opfer Christi und der Kirche zum Verständnis der Aussagen des Konzils von Trent," *Catholica* 41 (1977) 51–52.

26. E. J. Kilmartin, "The One Fruit and the Many Fruits of the Mass," *Proceedings of the Catholic Theological Society of America* 21 (1966) 43–50.

27. See *ibid.*, 50–52, for a discussion of John Duns Scotus' (d. 1308) contribution to this theme within a universalist ecclesiology.

28. *Ibid.*, 38: In the drastic revision of the *Regula canonicorum* of St. Chrodegang, bishop of Metz (743–66), it was determined that a priest should not take too many offerings. This rule presumed that the Mass was offered for the benefit of the individual donor of a gift to the exclusion of other donors.

29. The synod of Rome (826) opposed the practice of a priest's accepting the offering of one donor to the exclusion of others (see n. 22 above). Pope Alexander II (d. 1072) criticized the practice of multiplying Masses for money or flattery. Since Christ died once for all, the priest need not say one Mass for the day and another for the dead (Gratian, *Decretum* II, *De cons. dist.* 1, c. 53 [A. Friedberg, ed., Leipzig, 1879] 1308). Peter Damien (d. 1073) referred to the practice of offering Mass exclusively for one person and ridiculed the custom, for it gives the impression that Christ, who died for the salvation of the world, is now being offered up for the benefit of one individual (Opusc. 26, *Contra inscitiam et incuriam clericorum*, c. 2 (*PL* 145:501).

30. For example, in chapter 2 of the Acts of the Council of Lambeth (1281), it is asserted that a priest should not think that by celebrating one Mass he can satisfy for two for whom he promised *"in solidum celebrare"* (Mansi 24, 406–7). See Kilmartin, *op. cit.*, 49–50.

31. See K. Rahner and A. Häussling, *The Celebration of the Eucharist* (New York: Herder and Herder, 1968) 114–24; J. A. Jungmann, "Mass Intentions and Mass Stipends," in A. Kirchgaessner, ed., *Unto the Altar* (New York: Herder and Herder, 1963) 23–31; Kilmartin, *op. cit.*, 57–68, and "Money and the Ministry of the Sacraments," in W. Basset and P. Huizing, eds., *The Finances of the Church*. Concilium 117 (New York: Seabury Press, 1979) 104–11.

32. Flannery, *op. cit.*, 277.

33. *Encyclical Letter of Pope Pius XII on the Sacred Liturgy (Mediator Dei)* (Boston, St. Paul Editions, 1947) 39.

34. Flannery, *op. cit.*, 361.

35. *Ibid.*, 277.

36. Kilmartin, "Money and the Ministry of the Sacraments," 107–8.

37. Flannery, *op. cit.*, 277.

38. *Ibid.*

1. Bertolt Brecht, *The Good Person of Szechuan,* sc. 10; cited in J. Moltmann, *The Church in the Power of the Spirit* (New York: Harper & Row, 1977) 91.

2. I am referring to the specific Johannine usage that often carefully nuances "seeing" as a metaphor for responsive faith. See Raymond Brown's treatment of this usage, *The Gospel According to John (i–xii)* (Garden City, N.Y.: Doubleday, 1966) 501–3 (hereafter *John i–xii*).

3. *TDNT* 6:18.

4. John D. Crossan, *The Dark Interval: Towards a Theology of Story* (Niles, Ill.: Argus Communications, 1975) 54–57. Daniel O. Via, *The Parables: Their Literary and Existential Dimension* (Philadelphia: Fortress Press, 1967), would call this an example story, as distinguished from a parable (p. 12).

5. "The Rich Fool," *Heythrop Journal* 18 (1977) 131–51. I follow his analysis for the whole discussion of this parable.

6. *Ibid.,* 143–47.

7. *Ibid.,* 137–38, and esp. n. 36.

8. Joachim Jeremias, *The Parables of Jesus* (New York: Scribner's, 1963) 183. See John Navone, *Themes of St. Luke* (Rome: Gregorian University, n.d.) 100–117, for the context of parable in Lucan poverty.

9. *Ibid.,* 186–87.

10. John D. Crossan, *In Parables: The Challenge of the Historical Jesus* (New York: Harper & Row, 1973) 68. For the eschatological discussion of the parable of the rich fool, see Jeremias, *op. cit.,* 165; also H. Flender, *St. Luke, Theologian of Redemptive History* (Philadelphia: Fortress Press, 1967) 165–66.

11. Commenting on the parable of the rich man and Lazarus, Moltmann says: "The hidden presence of the coming Christ in the poor therefore belongs to ecclesiology first of all, and only after that to ethics" (*op. cit.,* 127).

12. For a detailed study of the two versions, see J. Dupont, *Les béatitudes: Le problème littéraire. Les deux versions du Sermon sur la montagne et des béatitudes* (Bruges: Abbaye de St. André, 1958) 218–23.

13. E. Schweizer, *The Good News According to Matthew* (Atlanta: John Knox Press, 1975) 91 (henceforth *Matthew*). For the covenant aspect, see K. H. Schelkle, "Das Herrenmahl," *Rechtfertigung. Festschrift für Ernst Käsemann zum 70 Geburtstag,* ed. J. Friedrich et al. (Tübingen: J.C.B. Mohr, 1976) 385–402, esp. 386–88.

14. See especially P. Lebeau, *Le vin nouveau du royaume* (Paris: Desclée de Brouwer, 1966) 19–52, for this whole discussion.

15. John L. McKenzie, *Second Isaiah: Introduction, Translation and Notes* (Garden City, N.Y.: Doubleday, 1968) 196–97.

16. *Ibid.,* 140. "But to accept the food of Yahweh as sufficient, and not to seek laboriously elsewhere for food that does not satisfy, is to commit oneself to faith in the saving power of Yahweh" (*ibid.,* 143).

17. J. Massyngberde Ford, *Revelation: Introduction, Translation and Commentary* (Garden City, N.Y.: Doubleday, 1975) 115; see also comments, 128.

18. L. Goppelt, "peinao," *TDNT* 6:22, n. 72. See also P. Borgen, *Bread from Heaven: An Exegetical Study of the Concept of Manna in the Gospel of John and the Writings of Philo* (Leiden: Brill, 1965) 179-92; R. Brown, *John i-xii*, 178-80; 247-48; 284-85; 292-93.

19. Mark 14, of course, is not exclusive. For the comparison of Johannine and Synoptic phrasing, see Brown, *John i-xii*, 285.

20. *The Prayers of Jesus* (Naperville, Ill.: A. Allenson, 1967) 100-102.

21. *Ibid.*, 102.

22. "If the feast of freedom is itself celebrated as a liberating feast, then it does take on the character of anticipation. . . . For the feast of freedom does not play with unreal possibilities but with the actual potentialities of the future of Christ in the creative Spirit" (Moltmann, *op. cit.*, 111). For the relationship between time, christology, and commitment, see *ibid.*, 75.

23. I have dealt with this problem of justification and need as symbolized in sacraments in my article "Of Reluctant Celebrants and Reliable Symbols," *Heythrop Journal* 18 (April 1977) 165-79.

24. *To Heal and to Reveal: The Prophetic Vocation According to Luke* (New York: Seabury Press, 1976) 61.

25. Again, Minear's analysis of the Lucan text, *ibid.*, 64.

26. See, for example, J. Jeremias, *New Testament Theology: The Proclamation of Jesus* (New York: Scribner's, 1971) 168-70; 247-49. For an example of how this biblical theme permeated early liturgy, see L. Clerici, *Einsammlung der Zerstreuten: Liturgiegeschichtliche Untersuchung zur Vor- und Nachgeschichte der Fürbitte für die Kirche in Didache 9, 4 und 10, 5* (Münster: Aschendorff, 1966) 65-102.

27. See, for example, Juan L. Segundo, *The Sacraments Today* (New York: Orbis Books, 1974) 104-10.

28. Jer 1:6-10. In a similar vein, see Minear, *op. cit.*, 70.

29. See the excellent article of E. Cothenet, "Prophétisme et le NT," *Supplément au Dictionnaire de la Bible* 8 (1972) 1308-11, 1326-31.

30. Prophecy is obviously being employed here in a broader (and more developed) meaning than the usual functional and classical one. I have no disagreement, then, with M. Hengel's contentions that Jesus was not "charismatic-prophetic" (*Nachfolge u. Charisma* [Berlin: Topelmann, 1968] 70-74). Hengel's eschatological emphasis in discipleship concurs with the approach taken here.

31. D. Daube, "Responsibilities of Master and Disciple in the Gospels," *New Testament Studies* 19 (1972) 1-15.

32. Mark 2:18ff.; Matt 9:14ff.; Luke 5:33ff.

33. Mark 2:23ff.; Matt 12:1ff.; Luke 6:1ff.

34. Mark 7:1ff.; Matt 15:1ff.

35. Mark 2:15ff.; Matt 9:10ff. (Mark 5:29ff. reverses the roles.)

36. For example, Joachim Jeremias, *New Testament Theology*, 116-18; L. Dussant, *L'Eucharistie, Pâques de toute la vie* (Paris: Editions du 1972) 87-121; and Jeremias' article "This Is My Body," *Expository Times* 83 (1973) 196-203, esp. 196-98.

37. I have presented an argument for sacrament as such (*in genere*) to be understood as *ot*, with specific reference to the Last Supper, in my article "Justification and Sacraments," *Journal of Ecumenical Studies* 16 (Fall 1979) 672–90. (See pertinent bibliography in that article, nn. 101–4.) H. Schürmann has made an unnecessary distinction between *ot* and "eschatological fulfillment-sign" to explain the Last Supper ("Das Weiterleben der Sache Jesu im nachösterlichen Herrenmahl," *Biblische Zeitschrift* 16 [1972] 1–23; here 18–20.)

38. *Pace* Moltmann, *op. cit.*, 247–49. It is not enough to say that "Jesus' fellowship of the common meal is therefore inseparable from his gospel of the nearness of the Kingdom and his acceptance of sinners" (*ibid.*, 248).

39. *Ibid.*, 249.

40. Mark 10:35–45; Matt 20:20–28. Schweizer (*op. cit.*, 297–98) correctly retrieves the context as that of "places of honor at the festal banquet. . . ."

41. Mark 16:14 is not our concern here.

42. B. Sandvik, *Das Kommen des Herrn beim Abendmahl im Neuen Testament* (Zürich: Zwingli, 1970) 23–27.

43. Cyrille Vogel, for example, has presented a well-substantiated argument from the practice of sacred meals of fish that would throw light on the post-Easter meals in Luke 24:41–43 and John 21:9–13 in "Le repas sacré au poisson," *Eucharisties d'Orient et d'Occident* (Paris: Editions du Cerf, 1970) 1:83–116. (This seems a more satisfying explanation than the usual apologetic one that Jesus thus proved he was not a ghost.)

44. See Raymond Brown, *The Gospel According to John (xiii–xxi)* (Garden City, N.Y.: Doubleday, 1970) 1093–1100, for a thorough coverage of the related problems (hereafter *John xiii–xxi*).

45. Lebeau, *op. cit.*, 113–15.

46. *Ibid.*, 126–27; 141.

47. Paul S. Minear, *Commands of Christ* (Nashville: Abingdon Press, 1972) 181.

48. J. H. Elliott, "Ministry and Church Order in the New Testament: A Tradition-Historical Analysis (I Pt. 5:1–5 and pars.)," *Catholic Biblical Quarterly* 32 (1970) 367–91; here 383.

49. See Brown, *John xiii–xxi*, 1112–17.

50. Jaques Ellul, *The Presence of His Kingdom*, cited in Minear, *To Heal and Reveal*, 122.

51. "This series of visions, auditions, covenantal promises and demands, by fulfilling earlier predictions and by issuing new assurances, served as a decisive reinterpretation of Scripture; it conveyed new understandings of Jesus' earlier work and a definite assignment for their own future work. . . ." (Minear, *ibid.*, 133).

52. In n. 40 above, the festal-banquet context of this scene was suggested. Together with the allusion to the cup of martyrdom (see E. Schweizer, *The Good News According to Mark* [Atlanta: John Knox Press, 1970] 218–19: henceforth cited as *Mark*), one might also argue for a more complex symbol: the cup of suffering *and* the festal meal-without-end.

53. Moltmann, *op. cit.*, 258.

54. Schweizer, *Matthew*, 264.

55. Fest: *The Transformation of Everyday* (Philadelphia: Fortress Press, 1976), 24ff.

56. *Ibid.*, 37.

57. "Theology and Praxis," *Cross Currents* 23 (1973) 154-68; here 167.

58. For the whole question, see M. Lamb, "The Theory-Praxis Relationship in Contemporary Christian Theologies," *Catholic Theological Society of America Proceedings* 31 (1976) 149-78.

59. "Religious symbols as lived are embedded in on-going life-worlds and before critical reflection can critique those symbols it must be adequately cognizant of the psychic, social, political, cultural and spiritual dynamics concretely affecting, and affected by, the religious symbols" (M. Lamb, *art. cit.*, 170, n. 72; also 171, n. 75).

60. Francis Fiorenza, "Critical Social Theory and Christology," *Catholic Theological Society of America Proceedings* 30 (1975) 63-110; here 104.

61. *Ibid.*, 104-7.

62. See, for example, Jürgen Habermas, *Theory and Practice* (Boston: Beacon Press, 1974) esp. 7-10.

63. The classic study remains W. Dürig, *Pietas Liturgica: Studien zum Frömmigkeitsbegriff und zur Gottesvorstellung der abendländischen Liturgie* (Regensburg: F. Pustet, 1958); see esp. 117-29.

64. R. Van Eynden, "Théologie: La foi sans religion chez Dietrich Bonhoeffer," *Faut-il encore une liturgie?* (Paris: Centurion, 1968) 131-54, esp. 148-54.

65. Segundo, *op. cit.*, 42-67. See also A. T. Hennelly, "The Challenge of Juan Luis Segundo," *Theological Studies* 38 (1977) 125-35.

66. P. Cornehl, "Öffentlicher Gottesdienst: Zum Strukturwandel der Liturgie," *Gottesdienst und Öffentlichkeit: Zur Theorie und Didaktik neuer Kommunikation* (Hamburg: Furche, 1970) 118-96.

67. Th. de Kray, "L'exégèse: religion et service de Dieu dans la Bible," in Van Eynden, *op. cit.*, 113-29, esp. 126-29.

68. I have developed these points in "Of Reluctant Celebrants and Reliable Symbols," *Heythrop Journal* 18 (1977) 165-79.

69. See Moltmann's strong position here, *op. cit.*, 88-89.

70. See Elizabeth Schüssler Fiorenza, *Priester für Gott: Studien zum Herrschafts- und Priestermotiv in der Apokalypse* (Münster: Aschendorff, 1972) esp. 343-44; and W. D. Hill, "On Suffering and Baptism in 1 Peter," *Novum Testamentum* 18 (1976) 181-89.

71. *Matthew*, 214.

72. *Ibid.*, 215.

73. J. E. Smith has given a fine statement of this; see his *Analogy of Experience* (New York: Harper & Row, 1973), 137-40.

74. This complements Moltmann's interpretation of Matt 25:31-46 ("I was hungry . . ."), where the needy are "the latent presence of the coming Savior and

Judge in the world, the touchstone which determines salvation and damnation"
(*op. cit.*, 127).

75. As cited by Roland de Vaux, *Studies in Old Testament Sacrifice* (Cardiff:
University of Wales, 1964) 24.